Creation

Problems in Theology

Creation

A Reader

Edited by
Jeff Astley, David Brown and Ann Loades

T & T CLARK
A Continuum imprint
LONDON • NEW YORK

T&T CLARK LTD
A Continuum imprint

The Tower Building   15 East 26th Street
11 York Road   New York, NY 10010
London SE1 7NX, UK   USA

www.continuumbooks.com

British Library Cataloguing-in-Publication Data
A catalogue record for this book is available from the British Library

ISBN 0 567 08977 0 (paperback)
ISBN 0 567 08978 9 (hardback)

Typeset by RefineCatch Limited, Bungay, Suffolk
Printed and bound in Great Britain by MPG Books Ltd, Bodmin, Cornwall

Contents

Preface

Courses in theology and religious studies in universities, colleges and sixth forms are increasingly 'topic-based' or 'problem-based', and usually form part of modular programmes of study for first degrees or AS/ A2 level qualifications. Teachers and students often find it difficult to access relevant primary material for the different topics that they have selected to study. Many textbooks are too general to be of more than limited value, and the same is true of selections of readings.

This series of readers in *Problems in Theology* is designed to meet this need by focusing on particular controversial themes and issues. Each volume provides a set of carefully selected readings from primary sources, together with a brief introductory essay, topics for discussion or further study, and a select bibliography. A particular advantage of the format adopted here is that teachers and students can use the material selectively, constructing their own educational pathway through the problem.

The readings chosen for these books have been tested out with undergraduate classes in the University of Durham. Much of this material will also be accessible, however, to sixth form students of religious studies, as well as to those studying theology on ordination courses and in adult education classes.

The editors wish to thank all who have assisted in this project by helping in the selection, referencing and trial-testing of material, by copytyping and editing the text, or by securing permissions. Particular thanks go to Paul Fletcher, Greta Gleeson, Evelyn Jackson and Declan O'Sullivan.

Notes on the text

The passages are printed (except for omissions, indicated by three full stops) as in the original text, with the same spelling, punctuation, etc. In most cases, however, notes within the readings have been omitted.

From time to time the editors have added their own explanatory comments. These are printed in italics and enclosed in square brackets.

Introduction

Reading the readings

According to the dictionary, creation is about making or bringing something into existence. In the Bible (see Reading 1.1) and in Christian thinking, however, creation is not just a bringing-into-being of the universe, but a care-full preserving of the universe in being, a maintaining and sustaining of all things. This continuing creation, 'the incessant act by which [God] preserves the world in existence',[1] implies the dependence of all beings – including human beings as free agents – on a continuing relationship with the Creator (1.4). Creation, a unique relationship between creature and Creator which expresses God's freedom and love, can only be spoken of in analogies and metaphors, including the narrative-metaphors of 'the creation myths' (1.1, 1.2, 1.3, 1.9; cf. 4.2).

Understood in these ways, the doctrine of creation is an expression of religious experience and attitudes, articulated as a theology. In no sense is it a scientific theory (see 1.5, 1.6, 4.5). The astrophysicist's cosmology (or 'cosmogony') that describes a Big Bang fifteen thousand million years ago and even earlier events, and the biologist's theory of the evolution of living species through natural selection, tell us about the origins and development of physical and biological Nature, but they do not go behind or beyond the natural world to its metaphysical origins and underlying meaning. Theology does, however, make claims about that further dimension; it 'offers us a personal-purposive, rather than a scientific-causal, explanation of the universe. It tells us about the purpose (the "why") of the world, not anything about what goes on within it (the "how")'.[2]

This division of labour between science and theology is expressed in

---

[1] Eric L. Mascall, *Christian Theology and Natural Science: Some Questions on their Relations*, London, SCM, 1956, p. 132.

[2] Jeff Astley, *God's World*, London, Darton, Longman & Todd, 2000, p. 3; see also Denis Alexander, *Rebuilding the Matrix: Science and Faith in the 21st Century*, Oxford, Lion, 2001, p. 307.

the distinction between what has been traditionally designated the independent and real 'secondary causality' of Nature, which operates in ways that fall under regular laws of Nature that may be investigated by science, on the one hand, and the divine creative activity, on the other. This second element is God's primary causation, which constitutes the 'uniform enabling of the secondary causes' power to act',[3] and provides Nature's ultimate explanation, purpose and point – its 'end' or 'final cause' (1.4, 1.5, 1.6, 1.9).

The evolution of living things through the operation of impersonal laws of Nature working on the products of chance variations (including genetic mutations and recombinations, and such unpredictable factors as environmental change) has seemed to many to remove *any* notion of design or purposefulness from Nature.[4] Others (e.g. Teilhard de Chardin, cf. 1.7, 3.2, 3.5), however, interpret evolution as the expression of a basically spiritual and directional process, an interpretation that appears more plausible now that a 'clockwork' form of total determinism within Nature is no longer supported by science and the universe may be viewed as a more open system, 'an emergent web of interacting energies'.[5] For some theologians, therefore, God may be found a place in Nature, with the universe open to the steering of God's providential influence without any need for abrupt, counter-natural interventions: 'the Spirit's action is hidden within the cloudiness of the intrinsically unpredictable' (1.8).

Such an interpretation of creation, and of God's purposive presence and activity within it, fits well with the picture painted by process theology. Alfred North Whitehead's metaphysics portrayed the universe as a community of events in flux, rather than as ultimately composed of static substances or things. The essential claim of process theology is that God is not the supreme exception to this, but its 'chief exemplification'. God changes too or (to be more accurate) God is 'dipolar', with both an 'eternal', 'absolute' aspect and a 'temporal', 'relative' one – the latter being God's 'consequent nature' that develops in relation to God's changing world. In this sense, God is 'consequent upon the world'[6] (2.1, 2.2). For Whitehead, however, if not for later process theologians, the world is not created out of nothing and has no beginning. Rather, it has always

---

[3] Maurice Wiles, *God's Action in the World*, London, SCM, 1986, p. 34.

[4] See, for example, Jacques Monod, *Chance and Necessity*, ET London, Collins, 1972; Richard Dawkins, *The Blind Watchmaker*, Harmondsworth, Penguin, 1991.

[5] Keith Ward, *God, Chance and Necessity*, Oxford, Oneworld, 1996, p. 57.

[6] David R. Griffin, 'Process Theology', in D. W. Musser and J. L. Price (eds), *A New Handbook of Christian Theology*, Cambridge, Lutterworth, 1992, p. 386.

existed alongside God, dependent on God for its existence and supremely influenced by God (cf. Cobb, 2.2).

As other readings in Chapter 2 reveal, some theologians have challenged process theology, in particular for setting up a straw man in its account of a 'monopolar' doctrine of God in contrast with its own 'neoclassical' theology, for its inadequate doctrine of creation and for privileging impersonal abstractions over personal analogies when speaking of God (2.3).

Colin Gunton has also criticized process theology for 'divinizing the world'. This is perhaps the gravest theological risk that faces those other perspectives, some of which are described in the readings in Chapter 3, that seek to develop a proper spirituality of the earth (3.1), including those that view God's relation to the world as one of panentheism[7] or the earth as 'the living Gaia' (3.2). These attempts at a 'green' or 'ecological' theology have many strengths, including the sense that humans are called to care for rather than dominate Nature (3.3, 3.4; cf. 4.6), but they also stand accused of sometimes downgrading humanity and even of sliding into pantheism (3.2, 3.5).[8] Theology needs always to affirm that God is 'beyond' as well as 'within' Nature; for the logic of creation implies that the Creator is not only immanently involved with but also, and necessarily, transcendent over the created world (that is, God is other than and different from the world) (cf. Tillich, 4.3).

In Chapter 4 we are reminded that Christian theology also needs to present a *Christian* doctrine of creation. As the biblical narratives and proclamations bear witness (1.1, 4.1, 4.3), creation is not separate from, but continuous with, God's intentions of redemption and fulfilment directed towards the human creation (1.4, 4.2). Creation is, above all, a redemptive act, and in Christianity redemption is always at the centre. Karl Barth is pivotal here, as a theologian who strove to overcome 'the unhappy tradition of distinguishing between creation and redemption' (Baum) by articulating a Christian doctrine of creation as creation *in*

---

[7] *Panentheism* is the belief that everything exists *in* God, so that the being of God may be said to encompass and include the world, while still transcending it. For Whitehead, 'the world lives by its incarnation of God in itself' (A. N. Whitehead, *Religion in the Making,* Cambridge, Cambridge University Press, 1926, p. 156), and for Arthur Peacocke God – like a mother – 'creates a world that is in principle and in origin other than him/herself but creates it, the world, within him/herself' (Arthur R. Peacocke, *Creation and the World of Science,* Oxford, Oxford University Press, 1979, p. 142). See also Tim Cooper, *Green Christianity: Caring for the Whole Creation,* Sevenoaks, Hodder & Stoughton, 1990, pp. 149–156.

[8] *Pantheism* is the belief that 'everything is God' and that God does not exist as separate from or more than the universe.

Christ (4.2, 4.3). His successors, while allowing more room than Barth did for a 'theology of Nature', have developed this Christological focus (1.2, 4.4, 4.6). Jürgen Moltmann's nuanced interpretation also takes up the archetypal symbol of rest and peace, the biblical image of the Sabbath – 'the feast of creation's redemption', to delineate the goal of creation (4.5). Theology may find here as fruitful a theme as it possesses in the better-known interpretation of the universe as 'sacramental' (4.6, 4.7). However it reads the world, Christian theology must always understand and approach it as the creation of the Christ-like God.

1 Creation

What does it mean?

1.1 Creation in the Old Testament

Genesis 1:1 to 2:4

1 ¹In the beginning when God created the heavens and the earth, ²the earth was a formless void and darkness covered the face of the deep, while a wind from God swept over the face of the waters. ³Then God said, 'Let there be light'; and there was light. ⁴And God saw that the light was good; and God separated the light from the darkness. ⁵God called the light Day, and the darkness he called Night. And there was evening and there was morning, the first day.

⁶And God said, 'Let there be a dome in the midst of the waters, and let it separate the waters from the waters.' ⁷So God made the dome and separated the waters that were under the dome from the waters that were above the dome. And it was so. ⁸God called the dome Sky. And there was evening and there was morning, the second day.

⁹And God said, 'Let the waters under the sky be gathered together into one place, and let the dry land appear.' And it was so. ¹⁰God called the dry land Earth, and the waters that were gathered together he called Seas. And God saw that it was good. ¹¹Then God said, 'Let the earth put forth vegetation: plants yielding seed, and fruit trees of every kind on earth that bear fruit with the seed in it.' And it was so. ¹²The earth brought forth vegetation: plants yielding seed of every kind, and trees of every kind bearing fruit with the seed in it. And God saw that it was good. ¹³And there was evening and there was morning, the third day.

¹⁴And God said, 'Let there be lights in the dome of the sky to separate the day from the night; and let them be for signs and for seasons and for days and years, ¹⁵and let them be lights in the dome of the sky to give light upon the earth.' And it was so. ¹⁶God made the two great lights – the greater light to rule the day and the lesser light to rule the night – and the stars. ¹⁷God set them in the dome of the sky to give light upon the earth,

[18]to rule over the day and over the night, and to separate the light from the darkness. And God saw that it was good. [19]And there was evening and there was morning, the fourth day.

[20]And God said, 'Let the waters bring forth swarms of living creatures, and let birds fly above the earth across the dome of the sky.' [21]So God created the great sea monsters and every living creature that moves, of every kind, with which the waters swarm, and every winged bird of every kind. And God saw that it was good. [22]God blessed them, saying, 'Be fruitful and multiply and fill the waters in the seas, and let birds multiply on the earth.' [23]And there was evening and there was morning, the fifth day.

[24]And God said, 'Let the earth bring forth living creatures of every kind: cattle and creeping things and wild animals of the earth of every kind.' And it was so. [25]God made the wild animals of the earth of every kind, and the cattle of every kind, and everything that creeps upon the ground of every kind. And God saw that it was good.

[26]Then God said, 'Let us make humankind in our image, according to our likeness; and let them have dominion over the fish of the sea, and over the birds of the air, and over the cattle, and over all the wild animals of the earth, and over every creeping thing that creeps upon the earth.' [27]So God created humankind in his image,
in the image of God he created them;
male and female he created them.

[28]God blessed them, and God said to them, 'Be fruitful and multiply, and fill the earth and subdue it; and have dominion over the fish of the sea and over the birds of the air and over every living thing that moves upon the earth.' [29]God said, 'See, I have given you every plant yielding seed that is upon the face of all the earth, and every tree with seed in its fruit; you shall have them for food. [30]And to every beast of the earth, and to every bird of the air, and to everything that creeps on the earth, everything that has the breath of life, I have given every green plant for food.' And it was so. [31]God saw everything that he had made, and indeed, it was very good. And there was evening and there was morning, the sixth day.

2 [1]Thus the heavens and the earth were finished, and all their multitude. [2]And on the seventh day God finished the work that he had done, and he rested on the seventh day from all the work that he had done. [3]So God blessed the seventh day and hallowed it, because on it God rested from all the work that he had done in creation.

[4]These are the generations of the heavens and the earth when they were created.

Job Chapters 38 and 39

38 1 Then the LORD answered Job out of the whirlwind:
2 'Who is this that darkens counsel by words without knowledge?

3 Gird up your loins like a man,
  I will question you, and you shall declare to me.
4 'Where were you when I laid the foundation of the earth?
  Tell me, if you have understanding.
5 Who determined its measurements – surely you know!
  Or who stretched the line upon it?
6 On what were its bases sunk,
  or who laid its cornerstone
7 when the morning stars sang together
  and all the heavenly beings shouted for joy?

8 'Or who shut in the sea with doors
  when it burst from the womb? –
9 when I made the clouds its garment,
  and thick darkness its swaddling band,
10 and prescribed bounds for it,
  and set bars and doors,
11 and said, 'Thus far shall you come, and no farther,
  and here shall your proud waves be stopped'?

12 'Have you commanded the morning since your days began,
  and caused the dawn to know its place,
13 so that it might take hold of the skirts of the earth,
  and the wicked be shaken out of it?
14 It is changed like clay under the seal,
  and it is dyed like a garment.
15 Light is withheld from the wicked,
  and their uplifted arm is broken.

16 'Have you entered into the springs of the sea,
  or walked in the recesses of the deep?
17 Have the gates of death been revealed to you,
  or have you seen the gates of deep darkness?
18 Have you comprehended the expanse of the earth?
  Declare, if you know all this.

19 'Where is the way to the dwelling of the light,
  and where is the place of darkness,

20 that you may take it to its territory
        and that you may discern the paths to its home?
21 Surely you know, for you were born then,
        and the number of your days is great!

22 'Have you entered the storehouses of the snow,
        or have you seen the storehouses of the hail,
23 which I have reserved for the time of trouble,
        for the day of battle and war?
24 What is the way to the place where the light is distributed,
        or where the east wind is scattered upon the earth?

25 'Who has cut a channel for the torrents of rain,
        and a way for the thunderbolt,
26 to bring rain on a land where no one lives,
        on the desert, which is empty of human life,
27 to satisfy the waste and desolate land,
        and to make the ground put forth grass?

28 'Has the rain a father,
        or who has begotten the drops of dew?
29 From whose womb did the ice come forth,
        and who has given birth to the hoarfrost of heaven?
30 The waters become hard like stone,
        and the face of the deep is frozen.

31 'Can you bind the chains of the Pleiades,
        or loose the cords of Orion?
32 Can you lead forth the Mazzaroth in their season,
        or can you guide the Bear with its children?
33 Do you know the ordinances of the heavens?
        Can you establish their rule on the earth?

34 'Can you lift up your voice to the clouds,
        so that a flood of waters may cover you?
35 Can you send forth lightnings, so that they may go
        and say to you, 'Here we are'?
36 Who has put wisdom in the inward parts,
        or given understanding to the mind?
37 Who has the wisdom to number the clouds?
        Or who can tilt the waterskins of the heavens,
38 when the dust runs into a mass
        and the clods cling together?

39 'Can you hunt the prey for the lion,
　　or satisfy the appetite of the young lions,
40 when they crouch in their dens,
　　or lie in wait in their covert?
41 Who provides for the raven its prey,
　　when its young ones cry to God,
　　and wander about for lack of food?

1 **39** 'Do you know when the mountain goats give birth?
　　Do you observe the calving of the deer?
2 Can you number the months that they fulfil,
　　and do you know the time when they give birth,
3 when they crouch to give birth to their offspring,
　　and are delivered of their young?
4 Their young ones become strong, they grow up in the open;
　　they go forth, and do not return to them.

5 'Who has let the wild ass go free?
　　Who has loosed the bonds of the swift ass,
6 to which I have given the steppe for its home,
　　the salt land for its dwelling place?
7 It scorns the tumult of the city;
　　it does not hear the shouts of the driver.
8 It ranges the mountains as its pasture,
　　and it searches after every green thing.

9 'Is the wild ox willing to serve you?
　　Will it spend the night at your crib?
10 Can you tie it in the furrow with ropes,
　　or will it harrow the valleys after you?
11 Will you depend on it because its strength is great,
　　and will you hand over your labour to it?
12 Do you have faith in it that it will return,
　　and bring your grain to your threshing floor?

13 'The ostrich's wings flap wildly,
　　though its pinions lack plumage.
14 For it leaves its eggs to the earth,
　　and lets them be warmed on the ground,
15 forgetting that a foot may crush them,
　　and that a wild animal may trample them.
16 It deals cruelly with its young, as if they were not its own;
　　though its labour should be in vain, yet it has no fear;

17 because God has made it forget wisdom,
and given it no share in understanding.
18 When it spreads its plume aloft,
it laughs at the horse and its rider.

19 'Do you give the horse its might?
Do you clothe its neck with mane?
20 Do you make it leap like the locust?
Its majestic snorting is terrible.
21 It paws violently, exults mightily;
it goes out to meet the weapons.
22 It laughs at fear, and is not dismayed;
it does not turn back from the sword.
23 Upon it rattle the quiver,
the flashing spear, and the javelin.
24 With fierceness and rage it swallows the ground;
it cannot stand still at the sound of the trumpet.
25 When the trumpet sounds, it says "Aha!"
From a distance it smells the battle,
the thunder of the captains, and the shouting.

26 'Is it by your wisdom that the hawk soars.
and spreads its wings toward the south?
27 Is it at your command that the eagle mounts up
and makes its nest on high?
28 It lives on the rock and makes its home
in the fastness of the rocky crag.
29 From there it spies the prey;
its eyes see it from far away.
30 Its young ones suck up blood;
and where the slain are, there it is.'

Isaiah 40:12–31, 42:5–9

12 **40**Who has measured the waters in the hollow of his hand
and marked off the heavens with a span,
enclosed the dust of the earth in a measure,
and weighed the mountains in scales
and the hills in a balance?
13 Who has directed the spirit of the LORD,
or as his counsellor has instructed him?
14 Whom did he consult for his enlightenment,
and who taught him the path of justice?

Who taught him knowledge,
and showed him the way of understanding?
15 Even the nations are like a drop from a bucket,
and are accounted as dust on the scales;
see, he takes up the isles like fine dust.
16 Lebanon would not provide fuel enough,
nor are its animals enough for a burnt offering.
17 All the nations are as nothing before him;
they are accounted by him as less than nothing and emptiness.

18 To whom then will you liken God,
or what likeness compare with him?
19 An idol? – A workman casts it,
and a goldsmith overlays it with gold,
and casts for it silver chains.
20 As a gift one chooses mulberry wood
– wood that will not rot –
then seeks out a skilled artisan
to set up an image that will not topple.

21 Have you not known? Have you not heard?
Has it not been told you from the beginning?
Have you not understood from the foundations of the earth?
22 It is he who sits above the circle of the earth,
and its inhabitants are like grasshoppers;
who stretches out the heavens like a curtain,
and spreads them like a tent to live in;
23 who brings princes to naught,
and makes the rulers of the earth as nothing.

24 Scarcely are they planted, scarcely sown,
scarcely has their stem taken root in the earth,
when he blows upon them, and they wither,
and the tempest carries them off like stubble.

25 To whom then will you compare me,
or who is my equal? says the Holy One.
26 Lift up your eyes on high and see:
Who created these?
He who brings out their host and numbers them,
calling them all by name;
because he is great in strength,
mighty in power,
not one is missing.

27   Why do you say, O Jacob,
     and speak, O Israel,
   'My way is hidden from the LORD,
     and my right is disregarded by my God'?
28   Have you not known? Have you not heard?
   The LORD is the everlasting God,
     the Creator of the ends of the earth.
   He does not faint or grow weary;
     his understanding is unsearchable.
29   He gives power to the faint,
     and strengthens the powerless.
30   Even youths will faint and be weary,
     and the young will fall exhausted;
31   but those who wait for the LORD shall renew their strength,
     they shall mount up with wings like eagles,
   they shall run and not be weary.
     they shall walk and not faint.

5   **42** Thus says God, the LORD,
        who created the heavens and stretched them out,
     who spread out the earth and what comes from it,
     who gives breath to the people upon it
       and spirit to those who walk in it:
6   I am the LORD, I have called you in righteousness,
       I have taken you by the hand and kept you;
     I have given you as a covenant to the people,
       a light to the nations,
7   to open the eyes that are blind,
     to bring out the prisoners from the dungeon,
       from the prison those who sit in darkness.
8   I am the LORD, that is my name;
       my glory I give to no other,
       nor my praise to idols.
9   See, the former things have come to pass,
       and new things I now declare;
     before they spring forth,
       I tell you of them.

Psalm 104:1–30

1   Bless the LORD, O my soul.
       O LORD my God, you are very great.

You are clothed with honour and majesty,
2   wrapped in light as with a garment.
You stretch out the heavens like a tent,
3   you set the beams of your chambers on the waters,
you make the clouds your chariot,
     you ride on the wings of the wind.
4   you make the winds your messengers,
     fire and flame your ministers.
5   you set the earth on its foundations,
     so that it shall never be shaken.
6   You cover it with the deep as with a garment;
     the waters stood above the mountains.
7   At your rebuke they flee;
     at the sound of your thunder they take to flight.
8   They rose up to the mountains, ran down to the valleys
     to the place that you appointed for them.
9   You set a boundary that they may not pass,
     so that they might not again cover the earth.

10   You make springs gush forth in the valleys;
     they flow between the hills,
11   giving drink to every wild animal;
     the wild asses quench their thirst.
12   By the streams the birds of the air have their habitation;
     they sing among the branches.
13   From your lofty abode you water the mountains;
     the earth is satisfied with the fruit of your work.

14   You cause the grass to grow for the cattle,
     and plants for people to use,
to bring forth food from the earth,
15   and wine to gladden the human heart,
oil to make the face shine,
     and bread to strengthen the human heart.
16   The trees of the lord are watered abundantly,
     the cedars of Lebanon that he planted.
17   In them the birds build their nests;
     the stork has its home in the fir trees.
18   The high mountains are for the wild goats;
     the rocks are a refuge for the coneys.
19   You have made the moon to mark the seasons;
     the sun knows its time for setting.

20   You make darkness, and it is night,
          when all the animals of the forest come creeping out.
21   The young lions roar for their prey,
          seeking their food from God.
22   When the sun rises, they withdraw
          and lie down in their dens.
23   People go out to their work
          and to their labour until the evening.

24   O LORD, how manifold are your works!
          In wisdom you have made them all;
          the earth is full of your creatures.
25   Yonder is the sea, great and wide,
          creeping things innumerable are there,
          living things both small and great.
26   There go the ships;
          and Leviathan that you formed to sport in it.

27   These all look to you
          to give them their food in due season;
28   when you give to them, they gather it up;
          when you open your hand, they are filled with good things.
29   When you hide your face, they are dismayed;
          when you take away their breath, they die
          and return to their dust.
30   When you send forth your spirit, they are created;
          and you renew the face of the ground.

[*Leviathan: a sea-monster, possibly a whale.*]

1.2 Making and emanation

John Macquarrie, *Principles of Christian Theology,* **London, SCM, 1966, pp. 200–3**

Christian theology has employed two models or analogues to elucidate the mystery of creation, and a consideration of these will help to clarify and expand our thinking about this theme. These models are 'making' and 'emanation.' The first of these is the fundamental one, taken from the Bible and developed through centuries of theological thought. The second has little foundation in the scriptures, but it entered into Christian theology at an early stage and has, as will be shown, its own value in correcting and supplementing the other model.

The image associated with the notion of 'making' is that of a craftsman producing an article for use. We have already noted that, like all analogues, this one is defective at certain points – it represents the relation between Being and the beings as a relation between beings, and it fails to express the notion of *creatio ex nihilo* [*that is, creation out of nothing*]. It is, however, the usual biblical analogy: 'God made the firmament'; 'God made the two great lights'; 'God made the beasts of the earth'; 'The Lord God made the earth and the heavens'; 'The Lord God formed man of dust from the ground'; 'The rib which the Lord God had taken from the man he made into a woman'; and so on (Gen. 1:7, 1:16, 1:25, 2:4, 2:7, 2:22). This analogy stresses the transcendence of God, who *makes* the world, whether directly as in the older creation myth or indirectly through his spoken word, as in the more sophisticated story. Thus the analogy also stresses the distance and the difference of being between God and the creatures. Furthermore, it represents the creation as a free act on the part of God.

The image usually associated with the notion of emanation is that of the sun sending forth its rays. As already said, this idea of creation is not very biblical, and often enough the ideas of emanation and creation are opposed to each other, though here we have chosen to oppose rather the ideas of emanation and making, subsuming both of them under the inclusive notion of creation. This procedure can be vindicated on the grounds that early Christian theologians such as Origen began to introduce the idea of emanation as interpretative of creation, and in one way or another the idea has continued to influence interpretation right down to our own time. It should not be regarded as a rival idea to the biblical one, or dismissed as extraneous because of its neo-Platonist provenance. It should indeed be regarded as secondary to the biblical idea, but as such it provides certain correctives and gives expression to insights that are not clearly presented in the image of making. Thus emanation suggests the immanence of God in the creation. It also stresses affinity and even closeness between the source and that which has sprung from it, though it certainly does not suggest for a moment that the creatures (the rays in the analogy) have anything like the same 'substantial' being as the Creator (the sun). Finally, it avoids the impression that creation could be considered like an arbitrary act, but it does this by moving too far in another direction and suggesting that creation is like a natural process.

I have outlined these two models of creation because I believe that their insights have to be combined. After all, whatever image we use will be inadequate, and there is a good case for correcting one image by another. If it is objected that in this case only one image seems to have a firm basis in the Bible, I think it can be replied that the other image too, though it must be subordinate to the first, does conserve insights that are scripturally based and has moreover been sanctioned by a long tradition of theological use from the Fathers to modern times.

Our teaching has been that Being combines its transcendence as the mysterious act of letting-be with its immanence as present-and-manifest in all particular beings. The image of making presents us with the idea of transcendent letting-be, but, unless it is suitably modified, it may entirely miss the idea of an immanent presence. The image of emanation insists on the other hand that God does really put himself into the creation, so that the risk of creation really matters to him, and he is really involved in it and concerned with it. Now, an image of pure emanation probably goes too far in this direction and leads us towards a pantheism in which all things are part of God, the human soul is a divine spark, and so on. This is certainly not Christian teaching yet the rejection of this extreme should not be allowed to blind us to the genuine truth for which a doctrine of emanation contends. Many writers have tried to find a middle position in thinking of the creation as analogous to a work of art, the point being that the artist really does put something of himself into such a work, while remaining external to it. But it may be doubted whether this does full justice to the immanence of God in the creation, or whether it expresses that degree of concern with and involvement in the creation that in the Christian religion finds its eventual expression in a doctrine of incarnation. It is all a question of maintaining a right balance of transcendence and immanence, and perhaps this is best done by holding side by side in their tension with one another the models of making and emanation.

These questions can be further opened up by considering creation in relation to the persons of the triune God. This matter has already come glancingly to our notice, and now we must pay some further attention to it.

Since the Father is primordial Being, the ultimate letting-be, it is natural that we should especially associate him with creation, and in the creeds he is specifically designated 'maker of heaven and earth'. The tendency to think of the Father as Creator to the point almost of equating the two is perhaps reinforced by our habit of thinking of creation so much in terms of the Old Testament narratives, to the neglect of what the New Testament says on the subject. This predominance of the Father in our thought of creation tends in turn to stress the divine transcendence and to lay a very heavy emphasis on the model of making. But the work of creation belongs to the triune God, and when we attend to the Son and the Holy Spirit in creation, this helps to redress the balance.

The New Testament speaks frequently of the Son or Logos as the agent through whom creation is effected. 'All things were made through him, and without him was not anything made that was made.' 'In him all things were created, in heaven and on earth, visible and invisible, whether thrones or dominions or principalities or authorities – all things were created through him and for him.' God 'has spoken to us by a Son, whom he appointed the heir of all things, through whom also he created the world' (John 1:3, Col. 1:16, Heb. 1:2). Many more quotations could be added, but these are enough to show that the teaching is clear and that it is common to several of the New Testament writers.

Now, we talked of the Son (Logos) as expressive Being, and it was pointed out that the traditional language which speaks of the Son in relation to the Father as 'generated' or 'begotten' preserves the unity of substance (Being) as between Father and Son, and is to be contrasted with the language of 'creating' which sets a difference between God and the creature. Expressive Being is not the creation, but the agent through which the creation comes into being. In other words, expressive Being is God in one of his ways of being; expressive Being is not the world, nor anything less than God. Yet it is precisely here that we have to find ways of expressing more adequately the immanence of God in the creation, for expressive Being, the outgoing life of God, is not only agent in creation but does really enter into creation. The combination in the Son transcendence and immanence is well expressed by St. Paul: 'He is before all things and in him all things hold together' (Col. 1:17). In the same passage, St. Paul has spoken of the Son as 'the first-born of all creation'. These questions belong to christology . . . but already – and not surprisingly – the christological center of the Christian faith is foreshadowed in our discussion of creation. God, we may say, is so intimately involved with his creation that in a remarkable way Creator and creature become one in the incarnation. But this can only be because the possibility (we might even be permitted to say, the purpose) is already there in creation, and in the transcendent-immanent relation between expressive Being and the beings.

1.3 On beginnings

Dietrich Bonhoeffer, *Creation and Temptation*, ET London, SCM, 1966, pp. 14–16

In the beginning – God. That is true if he is present to us in the middle with this word as the one who creates and not as one who is remote, reposing, eternally being. We can only *know* of the beginning in the true sense as we hear of it in the middle between beginning and end. Otherwise it would not be *the* beginning which is also our beginning. Of God as the beginning we know here in the middle, between the lost beginning and the lost end only – as of the Creator.

In the beginning God *created* the heavens and the earth. It does not say that first he was and then he created, but that in the beginning God created. This beginning is the beginning in the anxious middle and at the same time beyond the anxious middle where we have our being. We do not know of this beginning by stepping out of the middle and being in the middle ourselves. Only the lie could give us the power to do this, and therefore we would not be in the beginning but only in the middle and engulfed in the lie. We must bear in mind very clearly that we hear of the beginning only in the middle.

The twofold question arises: Is this beginning God's beginning or is it God's beginning with the world? But the fact that this question is asked is proof that we no longer know what 'beginning' means. The beginning can only be spoken of by those who are in the middle and are anxious about the beginning and end, by those who are tearing at their chains, by those – to anticipate something we shall discuss later – who only in their sin know that they are created by God. If this is so we can no longer ask whether this is God's beginning or God's beginning with the world. Luther was once asked what God was doing before the creation of the world. His answer was that he was cutting canes for people who ask such useless questions. This not only stopped the questioner short but also implied that where God is not recognized as the merciful Creator he must needs be known only as the wrathful judge, i.e. always in relation to the situation of the middle, between beginning and end. There is no possible question which could go back beyond this 'middle' to the beginning, to God as Creator. Thus it is impossible to ask why the world was created, about God's plan or about the necessity of creation. These questions are finally answered and disposed of as godless questions in the sentence, *In the beginning God created the heavens and the earth.* Not 'in the beginning God had this or that idea about the purpose of the world which we now only have to explore further', but 'In the beginning God *created*'. No question can penetrate behind God creating, because it is impossible to go behind the beginning.

From there it follows that the beginning is not a temporal distinction. We can always go behind the temporal beginning. But it is the truly unique thing that qualifies the beginning, not quantitively but in a qualitative sense – as something which simply cannot be repeated, which is completely free. We could conceive of a constant repetition of free acts, but this would be basically wrong because freedom does not repeat itself. If it did it would be freedom conditioned by freedom, in other words not freedom, and no longer the beginning.

This quite unrepeatable, unique, free event in the beginning, which must not be confused in any way with the year 4004 or any similar particular date, is the creation. *In the beginning God created the heavens and the earth.* That means that the Creator, in freedom, creates the creature. Their connexion is not conditioned by anything except freedom, which means that it is unconditioned. Hence every use of a causal category for understanding the act of creation is ruled out. Creator and creature cannot be said to have a relation of cause and effect, for between Creator and creature there is neither a law of motive nor a law of effect nor anything else. Between Creator and creature there is simply nothing: the void. For freedom happens in and through the void. There is no necessity that can be shown in God which can or must ensue in creation. There is nothing that causes him to create. Creation comes out of this void.

1.4 Continuous creation

Eric L. Mascall, *The Openness of Being: Natural Theology Today,* London, Darton, Longman & Todd, 1971, pp. 251–4

To many people the word 'creation' will simply suggest an act by which God is alleged to have brought the world or one of its constituents into existence at the beginning of its career, whenever that beginning may have been. The word is indeed sometimes used in this sense by theologians themselves, or at least by biblical scholars, as, for example, when the stories contained in the first two chapters of the book Genesis are described as 'creation-narratives'. In philosophical and dogmatic theology, however, 'creation' means much more than this, as is seen from the common assertion that it would still have application to finite beings even if they had always existed and therefore had no beginning at all. This can be illustrated very strikingly from the writings of St Thomas Aquinas, the greatest of the medieval theologians. St Thomas did in fact believe, in accordance with the interpretation of the Genesis stories which was current at his day, that the world had begun to exist at some particular date in the past and he was anxious to controvert the arguments of the Arab philosophers who claimed to prove by purely rational arguments, without any appeal to revelation, that the world had always existed and would always continue to exist. Nevertheless, he was convinced that reason itself could not settle the question; what was clear to him was that, whether the world had always existed or not, it must in either case be the creature of God. 'That the world did not always exist', he writes, 'is held by faith alone and cannot be proved by demonstration.' Everything except God is created, and to create is to make something out of nothing, but creation is no kind of change, for 'nothing' is not a being but the absence of any being. The creation of a being is in fact identical with its conservation. 'As it depends on God's will that he brings things into being, so it depends on his will that he keeps them in being; for he keeps them in being only by always giving them being. Therefore if he withdrew his action from them they would return to non-existence.' 'God causes this effect [*of being created*] in things, not only when they first begin to be but as long as they are kept in being.' For since God himself exists in eternity, creation is, from his standpoint, one timeless act by which the whole range of temporal existence is maintained in being; it is only from the temporal standpoint of the creature that creation is an act that begins when the creature begins. Nevertheless, *from the creature's standpoint* it is a continual and not a momentary act and it continues as long as the creature itself exists. It is important that this should be kept in mind in the subsequent discussion, as otherwise quite unnecessary difficulties will arise. The view that God's creative activity is involved only when a creature begins its career is a hangover from the discredited seventeenth- and eighteenth-century doctrine known as deism; it is certainly no part of traditional Christian teaching.

A more subtle but still important point is this; that creation is to be conceived as the imparting of being and not as the withholding of it. This assertion may sound cryptic and needs to be amplified. Some writers have thought it necessary, in order to protect the genuine freedom of the human will and to acquit God of direct responsibility for evil, to say that, within the sphere of the creature's freedom, God withholds his own activity. Thus Captain D. H. Doig, in a very interesting article on the problem of evil, has written as follows:

The act of divine creation must have something paradoxical about it. It cannot confer any benefit on God to create something, because he has the fulness of perfection already. And the first need must be for the Creator to withdraw his universality and omnipotence from a certain sphere in which his creation can operate. . . . Thus to express himself more fully he must surrender some freedom of action. His creation must be a positive act, but since it cannot add to what was already infinite, this must be balanced by a negative withdrawal.

(*Theology*, LXIX, 1966, pp. 485ff)

Now it must of course always be remembered that words taken from human experience and applied to God must be understood analogically, and it would be unfair to press the suggestions of the notion of withdrawal beyond its proper limits. Nevertheless, the notion that God has to withdraw himself from a certain sphere in order that, on balance, the totality of being shall not be augmented by the act of creation does not seem to me to be a happy one. The classical tradition of Christian theism would maintain that, simply because the creature is finite and God is infinite, the creature's existence, real as it is, does not add anything to the existence of God; no 'withdrawal' is necessary because there is no augmentation to be counterbalanced. So far from the creature's freedom implying a withdrawal of God from its sphere, that freedom is itself a gift of God and so implies God's entry into it, though 'entry', no less than 'withdrawal', is a radically analogous term. Where free-will is involved it seems to me much more satisfactory to start from the traditional assertion that God moves all secondary causes according to their natures: physical causes according to the nature of physical causes, and voluntary causes according to the nature of voluntary causes. For, although this is a statement of the problem rather than its solution, it is at least a statement of the right problem and not of the wrong one. It takes account of two truths of Christian experience: first, that when a man acts in accordance with God's will, God is not excluded from the act but is in fact the primary agent in it; secondly that when a man tries to exclude God from the act and make himself the primary agent, all that he manages to do is to introduce an element of sheer destruction and negation, an element which contravenes the man's own nature as fundamentally dependent upon God, an element which is not genuine activity but is rather deficiency in actuality, an element which goes against the creature's own inbuilt finality and is therefore self-frustrating and self-destructive. There is, I believe, deep truth and not mere slickness or paradox in the maxim that it is only in the order of negation and defect that the creature can be a primary cause. So long as he is acting in line with the authentic finality of the nature which God maintains in him he cannot keep God out, nor will he wish to do so. For the act by which the creature fulfils itself is simply the prolongation, in the finite realm of secondary causes, of the act by which God continually creates and conserves it. To try to exclude God from one's act is to repudiate one's ontological status as dependent upon God and so to frustrate oneself. In contrast, willingly to invite God as primary cause into one's act is not to abandon or diminish one's own freedom and spontaneity but to augment it. For in relations between persons, in contrast to relations between impersonal forces, provided the relations are authentically adjusted in accordance with the status and character of the parties, the influence of the one does not suppress but releases and enhances the freedom of the other; and this will be more and not less true when the former is the Creator himself. What I find unsatisfactory in Captain Doig's notion of 'withdrawal' is the suggestion that God withholds himself from the sphere in which he gives us freedom to act; rather I would wish to say that it is precisely by entering into it that he gives us freedom.

It should be unnecessary to add that the priority of God in this relationship is not a priority in time; it is not temporal but ontological. There is not an act of God, followed by an act of man; nor is there an act of man, followed by an act of God. There is one act, in which God is the primary cause and the creature is the secondary cause, and in which God exercises his primary cause by maintaining the creature's secondary causality and not by overriding or suppressing it.

1.5 First and final causes

Oliver Chase Quick, *Doctrines of the Creed: Their Basis in Scripture and Their Meaning Today*, London, Collins, 1963, pp. 45–7

We will begin then with the thought of God as creator. What do we mean by affirming that God is maker of heaven and earth?

In answering that question it is convenient to start from a provocative assertion made by a well-known modern writer: 'Darwin's *Origin of Species* is to-day a good deal more profitable as theology than the first chapter of Genesis.' To see the confusion of thought in this statement is to understand the difference between a theological doctrine of creation and a scientific doctrine of origins. Natural science is concerned with the causal order of events as they actually happen and have happened in space and time. This order, as it is traced backwards, brings us to certain primitive events which we may believe to have been the origin of life, or of the earth, or of the solar system or the stars. As to the nature and succession of these events it is doubtless true that the authority of such experts as Darwin is to be preferred to that of the author of Genesis. But theology is not interested primarily or chiefly in the question of temporal origins, even when it is stating its doctrine of creation. It is interested primarily and chiefly in the end or value of what has been created. In other words, it is only because of its interest in the final cause of things that theology is interested in the first cause at all. Now on the question of final cause, in any absolute sense, natural science has nothing whatever to say [*a final cause of something is its purpose or 'end'*]. Biology can indeed point out the relations of structure to function in organisms, and chemistry the peculiar adaptation of the terrestrial atmosphere which is needed to sustain life. Biology can even go further and show that man may in the future control the development of his own species in hitherto undreamed-of ways. But if you question the end and value of life itself, natural science is simply dumb. But just at this point, Genesis speaks with no uncertain voice. 'God saw everything that he had made, and behold it was very good.' That is the reason why 'in the beginning God created the heaven and the earth'. And to vindicate the belief that the world has a divine value the theologian attributes to it a divine origin. The value of the ultimate end must reveal the ultimate source. But when we speak of 'ultimate source' in this theological or metaphysical sense, it is obvious that we are speaking of something altogether beyond the series of spatio-temporal events with which alone natural science can deal. 'Thou madest us for thyself,' wrote St. Augustine, 'and our hearts are restless till they find rest in thee.' It is because the Christian believes himself to have been made for God, that he believes also that God made him. And the belief so grounded cannot be upset by anything that natural science may discover about the temporal origin of mankind.

Thus it appears that the expression 'first cause' is ambiguous in meaning. It may denote simply the event which comes temporally first in a causal series of events. Thus we may say that the falling of a spark is the first cause of a conflagration. When the expression is used in this sense, 'first causes' in the universe are investigated by natural science rather than by theology; and Darwin is more authoritative than Genesis. On the other hand, 'first cause' may denote the *explanation* of a process or series of events, i.e., that which causes it to exist as its reason or ground. Thus we may say that man's appreciation of music is the first cause of the construction of pianos. In this case it is obvious that the first cause is not itself a member of the series of events which constitutes the process explained. The appreciation of music is not one of the events which constitute the construction of a piano. It exists both before the process of construction begins and after it has ended. And in such a case the first cause is one with the final cause; for it is only purposive processes which can be thus explained. It is in some such sense as this that theology affirms God to be the first cause or creator of the world. Theology in its doctrine of creation takes us beyond the events of the process of world-history altogether to something which is in a fundamental sense their origin, because it directs the whole and explains it in terms of a value realized in its end.

1.6 Origins and ends, space and completion

John Polkinghorne, *Reason and Reality: The Relationship between Science and Theology*, London, SPCK, 1991, pp. 80–2

(a) *Origins* Perhaps no subject has given rise to more confusion in the interrelationship of science and theology than the question of how things began. It has often erroneously been supposed that the Christian doctrine of creation is principally concerned with initiation, with the primary instant. To think that is to confuse Christianity with deism. The doctrine of creation is concerned, not just with what God did, but with what he is doing; its subject is ontological origin, not temporal beginning. Its central assertion is that the physical world, at every instant of its existence, is held in being by the will of God. Two consequences follow. The first is that, if physical cosmology delivers us a dateable moment when the universe as we know it sprang forth from the Big Bang, that is scientifically very interesting but theologically neutral. There never was a theological stake in preferring big bang cosmology to steady state cosmology. Secondly, and conversely, if physical cosmology were to abolish a dateable beginning for the world, no great theological upheaval would follow. Stephen Hawking has proposed a highly speculative, but just conceivably correct, quantum cosmology in which the universe is a kind of fuzzy spacetime egg with no sharp beginning. He says, 'If the universe is really completely self-contained, having no boundary or edge, it would have neither beginning nor end; it would simply be. What place then for a creator?' It is theologically naive to give any other answer than 'every place' – as the ordainer and sustainer of the spacetime egg. God is not a God of the Edges, with a vested interest in boundaries.

. . .

(b) *The End* Cosmologists not only peer into the past but they can also attempt to descry the future. On the grandest scale, cosmic history is a tug of war between two opposing principles: the explosion of the big bang, throwing matter apart, and the pull of gravity, drawing matter together. They are very evenly balanced and we do not know which will win. Accordingly, we have to consider two alternative scenarios for the universe's future. If expansion wins, the galaxies will continue to fly apart for ever. Within themselves gravity will certainly win and they will condense into gigantic black holes, eventually decaying into low-grade radiation. That way lies cosmic death. The alternative scenario presents no more cheerful a prospect. If gravity wins, the present expansion will one day be halted and reversed. What began with the Big Bang will end with the Big Crunch, as the universe falls back into a singular cosmic melting pot. That way lies collapse.

On the face of it, the ultimate prospects are bleak. What does that imply for theology's claim that there is a purpose at work in the world? Christian orthodoxy has never subscribed to an evolutionary optimism which expects a total fulfilment of divine will to be brought about within the flux of present physical process. If there is a true and lasting hope – and it is a deep human intuition that there is such a hope – then it can only rest in the eternal mercy and faithfulness of God himself. Christians believe that for themselves (our bodies will decay on a time scale of tens of years) in their assertion of a destiny beyond death, and they can believe it as well for the whole universe (whose decay will be on a time scale of tens of billions of years). We need to embrace a cosmic hope as well as a personal hope, for it would be far too anthropocentric simply to regard this vast universe as being of concern to God only as the backdrop for a human drama which has just started after an overture lasting fifteen billion years. It is, of course, beyond our feeble powers of imagination to conceive what that act of cosmic redemption will be like, but if there is a true hope it lies in God and not in physics.

Jürgen Moltmann, *God in Creation: An Ecological Doctrine of Creation*, ET London, SCM, 1985, pp. 156–7, 193

The problem which was discussed between Leibniz and Newton can, in my view, only be solved if we think of creation as the mediation between the relative space of objects and the eternal space of God. It is only the concept of creation which distinguishes the space of God from the space of the created world; for with creation, a space for the created world comes into being which is neither the uncreated omnipresence of God nor, as yet, the relative space of objects. Although Max Jammer discussed this 'Jewish-Christian idea of space', he failed to perceive the possible solution it essentially offers for the dispute between Leibniz and Newton. 'According to the Cabala', he writes, 'the Infinite Holy One, whose light originally occupied the whole universe, withdrew his light and concentrated it on his own substance, thereby creating empty space.' This is the doctrine of the divine *zimsum*. Kabbalistic interpreters [*from the mediaeval Jewish mystical tradition*] surmised that this is why Genesis does not talk about the creation of space; for it is rather that creation is fashioned *in* the emptiness God ceded for it through his creative resolve. So the space of creation precedes both creation and the spaces fashioned within creation, yet without being identical with the uncreated, eternal omnipresence of God. 'After God, in his resolve to create the world, had completed the *zimsum*, he created "vessels". He set them in "the place" which he had made free for them through his withdrawal. These vessels were destined to receive the light in which the world was to spring to life.'

The created world does not exist in 'the absolute space' of the divine Being; it exists in the space God yielded up for it through his creative resolve. The world does not exist in itself. It exists in 'the ceded space' of God's world-presence. It is not the eternal God himself who is the boundary of the world, as Newton seems to think. It is God the Creator. In the doctrine about the world as God's creation we therefore distinguish between three things: first, the essential omnipresence of God, or *absolute space*; second, *the space of creation* in the world-presence of God conceded to it; and third, *relative places*, relationships and movements in the created world. The space of the world corresponds to God's world-presence, which initiates this space, limits it and interpenetrates it.

. . .

In the dispute about that part of evolutionary theory which is concerned with the descent of man, the Christian doctrine of creation came to be narrowed down to creation in the beginning (*creatio originalis*); and this was further contracted still to the aspect of God's creative activity. The doctrine of the divine 'making', the doctrine of continuous creation (*creatio continua*) and the doctrine of the new creation still to be consummated (*creatio nova*) all receded into the background and were forgotten. As a result, creation in the beginning was declared to be a finished and complete creation, capable of no history and in need of no evolution. The human being too, created to be 'the image of God', was viewed as a being created once and for all, and therefore finished and complete; he was not a being intended for evolution. Finally, the relation between God and his creation was restricted to a relation of causality, and the wealth of God's other relationships to the world, and the world to him, was disregarded. These ideas were put forward in an attempt to vindicate the doctrine of creation. But in fact they only succeeded in tying the picture of God's creation inexorably to the notions about the static [cosmos] which were current coin in the Christian middle ages. The contradictions between the biblical belief in creation and the ancient world's veneration for the cosmos were overlooked; though these contradictions had in fact remained unresolved in the mediaeval synthesis.

1.7 Evolution, chance and direction

Ian G. Barbour, *Issues in Science and Religion*, London, SCM, 1966, pp. 89–90, 399–402

The prevalent version of the argument from design was particularly vulnerable, for it had started from the observed *adaptation of organic structures to useful functions*. But such adaptation could be accounted for by natural selection without invoking any preconceived plan. Usefulness was an effect and not a cause; it was the end product of an impersonal process. The species in existence are present simply because they have survived while thousands of others lost out in the struggle for existence. Instead of marveling that a fish has an eye that can see under water, we should have reason to be surprised only if this were *not* the case. Moreover, some of the facts that had always created difficulties for the advocates of design – such as useless rudimentary organs and traces of long-vanished limbs – could now be readily explained.

In some of his writings Darwin expressed the view that the *laws* by which life evolved were created by God, though the particular species resulting were the product of *chance* rather than design:

There seems no more design in the variability of organic beings and in the action of natural science than in the course which the wind blows. Everything in nature is the result of fixed laws. . . . On the other hand, I cannot anyhow be contented to view this wonderful universe, and especially the nature of man, and to conclude that everything is the result of brute force. I am inclined to look at everything as resulting from designed laws, with the details, whether good or bad, left to the working out of what we may call chance.

Chance seemed to be the antithesis of design. Darwin assumed that organic change is the product of a very large number of random spontaneous variations occurring entirely independently of each other, so the final result is accidental and unpremeditated. But the element of lawfulness, which received greater emphasis than the idea of chance, was also understood in a way which denied design. To earlier generations, scientific laws expressed the wisdom and constancy of God and were instruments of his purposes. Now they were increasingly taken as the autonomous and mechanical operation of impersonal forces. Law as well as chance appeared to be blind and purposeless.

Darwin at one point indicated that lawfulness does not exclude the concept of God *as primary cause*; he even spoke of natural laws as the 'secondary means' by which God created. He came close to recognizing that the scientist studies the domain of secondary causes and cannot ask why nature works as it does. But the following passage suggests that his own epistemology was undermined by the admission of the lowly origins of man's mind, so that in his later years he took a more agnostic position. He maintains:

. . . the impossibility of conceiving this immense and wonderful universe, including man with his capacity for looking far backwards and far into futurity, as the result of blind chance or necessity. When thus reflecting I feel compelled to look to a First Cause having an intelligent mind in some degree analogous to that of man: and I deserve to be called a Theist. . . . But then arises the doubt, can the mind of man, which has, as I fully believe, been developed from a mind as low as that possessed by the lowest animals, be trusted when it draws such grand conclusions.

Neither in the typical formulations of the design argument, such as Paley's, nor in the rejection of it by Darwin and others of his time, was the nature of divine causality discussed. Usually God's activity had simply been assumed to be like that of a workman; and evolution made this simple 'maker' analogy untenable.

. . .

The Jesuit paleontologist Teilhard de Chardin has powerfully expressed a vision of an evolutionary process which is basically spiritual in character . . . His thought was developed with an independence – even in coining words of his own – that precludes assigning him to any school of thought. In *The Phenomenon of Man*, scientific data from many fields are presented within a total coherent synthesis of magnificent sweep and vivid imagery. Such a book cannot be summarized, but we can paraphrase three concepts relevant to our discussion:

1. *The continuity of the levels of reality*. Teilhard traces four stages of evolution (matter, life, thought, society) that are continuous with each other. His fundamental sense of the coherence of the universe leads him to picture 'a single process without interruption,' an integral development without gaps. Each level has its roots in earlier levels and represents the flowering of what was potentially present all along. The higher is already existent in the lower in rudimentary form: 'In the world, nothing could ever

burst forth as final across the different thresholds successively traversed by evolution (however critical they be) which had not already existed in an obscure and primordial way. . . . Everything, in some extremely attenu- ated version of itself, has existed from the very first' (pp. 71, 78). There is no sharp line between the nonliving and the living; there could be no life unless there was already incipient life in all matter. Similarly there is no line between life and thought; mindlike activity of an elementary kind reaches all the way down the scale of life, though it becomes impercept- ible, 'lost in darkness,' as we trace it back. Teilhard does not, of course, impute self-consciousness or reflection to lower organisms; their 'psy- chic life' is infinitesimal, but represents the beginnings of perception, sensitivity, and spontaneity. He assigns great importance to this inner aspect, the *'within of things,'* which finally developed into mind. From our knowledge of ourselves we can reason that 'since the stuff of the uni- verse has an inner aspect at one point of itself, there is necessarily a double aspect to its structure, that is to say in every region of space and time.' Here is a theme reminiscent of Whitehead.

But Teilhard also maintains that there have been a number of *thresh- olds* or *critical points*. These 'crises' were not gaps or absolute dis- continuities, but each marked a crucial breakthrough to a new level. Though the levels interpenetrate, there was real novelty in each new beginning (the word 'emergence' is occasionally used). This idea of a critical point within a continuous process is vividly conveyed by the metaphors with which the book's second section closes, after the main branches (phyla) of primate evolution have been traced to the very threshold of reflective thought:

We already knew that everywhere the active phyletic lines grow
warm with consciousness toward the summit. But in one well-
marked region at the heart of the mammals, where the most powerful
brains ever made by nature are to be found, they become red hot.
And right at the heart of that glow burns a point of incandescence.

We must not lose sight of that line crimsoned by the dawn. After
thousands of years rising below the horizon, a flame bursts forth at a
strictly localized point.

Thought is born. (p. 160)

2. *The directionality of evolution*. There has been a trend toward greater *complexity* and greater *consciousness*. The increasing outward complex- ity of the nervous system and brain is correlated with the inward ascent to reflective thought. There is also a tendency toward personalization and

individuation that is significant in any extrapolation to the future. One of the most original aspects of Teilhard's thought is his idea of *convergence* at each evolutionary stage. He pictures phases of expansion, radiation, and diversification followed by phases of consolidation, unification, and 'involution.' Though human societies at first diversified, they are now converging toward interdependence and unification, which will lead to a single 'inter-thinking' fabric of humanity. But Teilhard holds that despite directionality there has been much *groping* along the way. He speaks of the brutality of the process, its wastefulness, indifference to the individual, and excursions into blind alleys. 'Groping' seems to imply a constant goal but a diversity of short-run directions. He defines it as 'directed chance', 'the blind fantasy of large numbers combined with the precise orientation of a specific target.'

Teilhard apparently holds that *mutation* and *natural selection* play important roles in this directionality. 'The universe . . . proceeds step by step by dint of billionfold trial and error. It is this process of groping combined with the twofold mechanism of reproduction and heredity, allowing the hoarding and additive improvement of favorable combinations' which produces progress. The final outcome is uncertain because of 'chance at the bottom and freedom at the top.' The ability to use chance opportunities is in part a function of the internal life of the individual organism (instinct, intelligence and the like); but *the within of things* also appears to be a channel for a transindividual upward striving that takes advantage of chance:

> The impetus of the world, glimpsed in the great drive of consciousness, can only have its ultimate source in some *inner* principle which alone would explain its irreversible advance toward higher psychisms. . . . The long-term modifications of the phylum are as a rule so gradual, and the organs affected are sometimes so stable . . . that we are definitely forced to abandon the idea of explaining every case simply as the survival of the fittest. (pp. 149–50)

3. *The convergence of evolution to the Omega Point*. An essential theme in Teilhard's message is the incompleteness of evolution. Creation is continuing; the universe is still in the process of being born. The social stage is moving toward a higher synthesis, the unification of mankind into a collectivity of consciousness, a global confluence into a single inter-thinking unit. This communal destiny of socialization into a kind of super-organism can be achieved without the loss of individuality which occurs

in insect societies or totalitarian states. For the new humanity will
maintain the integrity of personality, and its bond of union will be love.

1.8 Determinism, openness and the Spirit

The Doctrine Commission of the General Synod of the Church of
England, *We Believe in the Holy Spirit*, London, Church House
Publishing, 1991, pp. 135–6, 140–3

The Bible begins with creation stories expressed in terms of the cosmologies of their day. It must surely be our purpose to make similar use
of the vastly better informed cosmology, now available to us. Other
sources of creation theology in the Old Testament include Second Isaiah
(perhaps influenced by contact with the astronomically quite sophisticated culture of Babylon) and the Wisdom writers (who in their cool
appraisal of the world around them represent the nearest that ancient
Israel got to a 'scientific' tradition). The prologue of John's Gospel relates
the creation of all things to the action of the *Logos*. One of the concepts
constellated around the Word is that of rational order. There is, therefore,
encouragement from 'the book of scripture' to attempt to read 'the book
of nature' with all due seriousness.

Science has an impressive story to tell about cosmic history. In brief
we may say that just as man emerged through biological evolution, so the
earth emerged from the ashes of dead stars, which in their turn emerged
from the hydrogen and helium formed in the first three minutes of the
universe's history, a history which in the shortest instants following on
the fiery explosion of the Big Bang (if we are to believe the boldest specu-
lations of the cosmologists) had already seen a sequence of remarkable
transformations in the nature of cosmic actuality. Cosmologists are able
to attempt to speak of the universe when it was only a fraction of a
second old because it was then so simple and undifferentiated in its
structure – at one stage an almost uniform energetic soup of elementary
particles, for instance. Yet, over a fifteen-billion-year history, that initial
simplicity has evolved systems as complex and interesting as ourselves.
Out of stardust has come humankind, beings capable of self-
consciousness and spiritual awareness. To speak thus is by no means to
embrace a reductionist account. The history of cosmic evolution appears
continuous. Scientific inspection reveals no need to postulate the injec-
tion of a new ingredient before humankind could come to be, but that
history is open to an interpretation emphasizing the need to consider
entities in their totality, within which humanity can be recognized as novel

and unique. 'Mere matter' (as it might have seemed) has proved to be endowed with an astonishing degree of fruitfulness. That from the processes of the universe have emerged creatures capable of understanding the cosmos is a profound and moving mystery.

. . .

Any creative activity, bringing about that which is new, requires for its possibility that there is an openness in what is going on. Otherwise the future is just a rearrangement of what was already existing in the past, with no intrinsic novelty. In a purely mechanical universe there is no true development. Pierre Simon Laplace, the greatest of Newton's successors, conceived of a demon calculator who, knowing the present positions and velocities of all the atoms in Newtonian world, could immediately predict the whole future and retrodict the whole past. In such a universe there would be no becoming. Time would be just an index of where one is along the tramline, not a measure of how such a universe has evolved.

There is something fishy about Laplace's picture, particularly when applied to himself. We should take with the utmost seriousness our intuition that we enjoy some room for manoeuvre within the flux of what is going on. It is a basic human experience that our futures are to some degree open. In the science of the twentieth century we have come to see that the physical world is indeed different from the way that Laplace thought about it. Partly this is due to quantum theory's abolition of precise determinism, though that is almost always only of significance for small-scale events at the atomic level or below. Much more significant for our present purpose is the fact that the theory of dynamical instabilities (the theory of chaos, as it is called) has made it plain that even Newtonian systems are far from being generally susceptible to tight prediction and control. This is due to the exquisite sensitivity that these systems display in relation to the minutest variation in their circumstance. (In a crude way this will be familiar to any snooker player!) In terms of a metaphor of Karl Popper, the universe proves to be composed of (unpredictable) clouds with only a few (predictable) clocks among them.

Laplace had supposed that his demon possessed exact knowledge of everything that is happening. It would have seemed reasonable to suppose that if that knowledge were not quite exact, then the predicted consequences would also not be quite exact, but to a degree that was contained within tolerable limits. A key discovery has been that in general this is not true. Instead, for complex dynamical systems, initial circumstances which differ from each other by only infinitesimal amounts lead to subsequent motions which diverge from each other to arbitrary degrees. One of the earliest discoveries in this area arose from the study of computer models of the weather. This is 'only half-jokingly known as the Butterfly Effect – the notion that a butterfly stirring the air today in Peking can transform storm systems next month in New York' (J. Gleick, *Chaos* p. 8). When we are concerned with systems of such delicate sensitivity, the smallest fluctuations can trigger substantial consequences.

Intrinsic unpredictability is concerned with what we can know, but it gives us unforced encouragement to go on to an option about what we believe to be the case, taking a more supple view of reality than that provided by the Laplacian straitjacket. At last a picture of the physical world is available in which there seems some degree of consonance in thinking of ourselves as among the inhabitants of the world. Its unpredictable flexibility is congruent with our experience of openness. That flexibility is not confined to living beings; the process of the universe is shot through with it. Thus there seems also the possibility for the working of the Spirit within the whole cosmic process.

It is important to be clear about what is being said. We are not claiming anything so extravagant as that the age-old problems of divine and human action are solved in detail. We simply record the death of a merely mechanical view and the birthpangs of a physics able to speak of both being *and* becoming. The openness that characterizes the modern theory of dynamical systems is due to those systems having, in their temporal development, to thread their way through a labyrinth of proliferating bifurcating possibilities. One can get some feel for what is involved by thinking of the very simplest model of a single bifurcation. Consider a bead threading a perfectly smooth wire in the shape of an inverted U. The bead rests at the top of the wire. The tiniest 'nudge' will displace it to one side or the other, and according to which way it is displaced the bead will fall either to right or to left. Thus infinitesimal triggers produce widely contrasting outcomes (way over to the right or way over to the left), in which no transaction of energy is required (the smallest displacement will do the trick if the wire is perfectly smooth). [See illustration overleaf.]

Of course, we are concerned, not with beads on wires, but with the abstract structure of possibility illustrated by this simple system. It turns out that complex dynamical systems evolve through endless bifurcations, the negotiation of which involve zero-energy exchange but which result in non-zero difference in consequent behaviour (the bead falls to the right or to the left). This crude and simple parable may help us to consider the feasibility of the Spirit's action within the almost infinite variety and open flexibility of cosmic process. The picture is not of

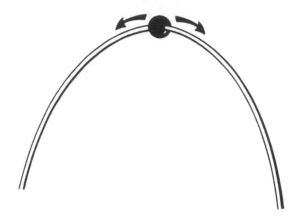

energetic causation (the Spirit is not an agent among other physical agencies) nor of arbitrary intervention in gaps (there is no suspension of the operation of those physical laws whose regularities the theist will see as reflections of divine faithfulness) but of a guiding within the *inherent* openness of the flux of becoming. Necessarily the Spirit's action is hidden within the cloudiness of the intrinsically unpredictable. There is, of course, no interference with those occurrences (such as the succession of the seasons) which do enjoy a clockwork regularity. We believe that modern physical theory is entirely consonant with theological discourse of the Spirit at work 'really on the inside'.

We do not attempt to breach the hiddenness by attempting to spell out any detailed conjectures of how the Spirit has been working. A modern scientific writer has said about the universe, 'There exists alongside the entropy arrow (the direction of decay) another arrow of time, equally fundamental, and no less subtle in nature . . . I refer to the fact that the universe is progressing – through the steady growth of structure, organisation and complexity – to ever more developed and elaborate states of matter and energy'. The writer goes on to refer to this increase in organisation as 'an objective fact' (P. Davies, *The Cosmic Blueprint*, p. 20). Teilhard de Chardin called this fact complexification. The universe started extremely simple and uniform. It has become remarkably differentiated, with highly structured subsystems (such as ourselves). There is no reason to suppose that this process is not susceptible to discussion in scientific terms – indeed the quotation above is taken from a book which is about such topics as the theory of complex dynamical systems. But since science is discerning processes intrinsically open in their character, there is no reason to deny to theology the right to its own point of view, as it seeks to understand the evolving fruitfulness of the universe in terms of the patient and subtle operation of the Spirit on the inside of physical process.

1.9 Creation, myth and theology

David Brown, *Invitation to Theology*, Oxford, Blackwell, 1989, pp. 12–14

Although the Bible opens in this mythological way, central rather to the Old Testament view of God is the idea of God's action in history and his involvement with a particular people. The theme of creation is seldom to be found in any explicit form, and in fact the Bible's opening story of the creation is a late response to, and adaptation of, an already existing Babylonian myth. This is important to note because, though most primitive peoples do have some form of creation myth, it would be quite wrong to suggest that puzzling about how the world began is what makes them 'theologians'. Such a view would equate theology with primitive science. Of course religion did sometimes function like that, as with the use of demons to explain the existence of physical illness, but to see that as central would be to misunderstand totally the aims of religious thinking. What was being explored through myth was a meaningful framework in terms of which one could intelligibly relate to the world and respond to it. Thus, in so far as the question of creation was raised, it was raised as a way of considering what the world now is like, not what it was like when it began. So even in creation myths the interest was not in causal explanations but in a search for meaning, a framework in terms of which life could be lived.

This is beautifully illustrated by that opening chapter, and the alterations the author makes. Scholars call him P because he is believed to have been a priestly editor (or editors) of the Pentateuch (the first five books of the Bible), writing about 500 BC, who sometimes incorporates his sources unchanged, sometimes adds material of his own, and sometimes – as in this case – reworks earlier pagan accounts. The original Babylonian myth, called *Enuma Elish*, had presented a rather negative view. The world's creation was due to conflict, a battle between the gods. P retains various mythological elements such as the divisions of days and God 'resting' on the seventh day, but at the same time removes all the negative import of the myth. The defeated goddess Tiamat, the chaos monster out of whom the cosmos was created by the god Marduk, survives only as the *tehom*, the related Hebrew word for the unformed watery chaos. The point being made is that the world is good (repeatedly affirmed in the declaration 'and God saw that it was good') and not a battleground of the gods. Indeed, so little is the writer concerned to offer a causal explanation that no account is given of how the *tehom* came into existence, and we must await that for several centuries until the apocryphal 2 Maccabees (7:28). Indeed, even well into the Christian era some of the Church Fathers, for example Justin Martyr and Clement of Alexandria, still saw no need for a doctrine of divine creation out of nothing.

Our point can be carried further by observing that modern scholarship reveals that P has combined his account with an earlier version that begins at Genesis 2:4 in a way that indicates that causal explanation could not have been his primary aim. For once one compares the two chapters closely, the inconsistencies are clearly to be seen, with, for example, plants appearing later than man in the earlier account (2:19–20), or again woman being created separately from man (2:22) rather than simultaneously as in the later version (1:26–7). Either we have to say that P was a rather poor editor (in addition to producing his own material he introduced elements from sources known as J, E and D) or, surely more probably, we must recognize that for him such inconsistencies did not matter, because giving an account of the origins of the cosmos was not the objective with which he was writing. In other words, it was a matter of complete indifference to him when and how the plants arrived. What mattered was that they were good and part of an ordered, structured universe in which God had a plan and purpose for man.

I hasten to add that I am not denying that myths were sometimes invented to give an explanation. Indeed, there is a whole category of them concerned with the explanation of the origin of the names of peoples and places. They are called aetiological myths, and examples can be found in the Bible, as in the story in Genesis 32:24ff of Jacob (Hebrew = 'the supplanter') wrestling with God and being renamed Israel (Hebrew = 'perseverer with God'). But even here the reason why J chooses to tell the story is ultimately theological, that Jacob who had cheated his elder brother of his rightful blessing has at last won through by his perseverance and been blessed by God. The mythical story is merely seen as symbolizing this.

Topics for discussion

1 What do we mean by creation? How helpful are making, emanation and/or artistic work as analogies? Is it a doctrine about the world's beginnings or origin, or about its present or future existence, or what?
2 What is the difference between first cause as ultimate source and first cause as beginning?
3 How should theology regard scientific accounts of the beginning and end of the world? Do they necessitate any modifications to Christian doctrine?
4 To what extent should Darwin's theory of evolution be seen as undermining a divine creative role? How plausible do you find Teilhard de Chardin's re-expression of evolution in religious terms?
5 What is the difference between myth, theology and science? If one calls Genesis 1 a myth, does this imply an inferior kind of truth?
6 Could a more developed doctrine of the Holy Spirit bridge talk of God and talk of the natural world?

2 Process theology

A more engaging God?

2.1 Overview: A dynamic God

David Brown, *Continental Philosophy and Modern Theology: An Engagement*, Oxford, Blackwell, 1987, pp. 49–51

Process Theology . . . seeks to replace the static notion of substance that has dominated theology for so long with a dynamic notion of God as process. The actual term 'process theology' seems only to have gained currency in the fifties, though its antecedents are much older than that. The Cambridge mathematician and philosopher A. N. Whitehead (1861–1947) is the seminal influence. During his fellowship at Trinity he collaborated with Bertrand Russell on *Principia Mathematica*, but by the time he produced *Process and Reality* he had already accepted a professorship of philosophy at Harvard. There Charles Hartshorne was one of his assistants. In 1928 Hartshorne moved to the philosophy department at the University of Chicago, where he remained until 1955. It was largely thanks to him that Whitehead's often difficult ideas were popularized in theology, and by the sixties a whole stream of books were appearing on the subject, of which John Cobb's *A Christian Natural Theology* and Schubert Ogden's *The Reality of God* are typical.

The basic idea of what Whitehead calls his 'philosophy of organism' is that science reveals to us that all reality is in movement and that being so we are not entitled to make God an exception. Thus, despite Newton's discovery, *contra* Aristotle, that motion was no less natural than rest, Whitehead upbraids him for not carrying his insight far enough. Newton in his *Scholium* had accepted notions of absolute space and time, whereas Plato in his *Timaeus*, he claims, saw the essential point of universal growth. 'The full sweep of the modern doctrine of evolution would have confused the Newton of the *Scholium*, but would have enlightened the Plato of the *Timaeus*.' Other contrasts to which Whitehead points in Plato's favour are the way in which his preference for mathematical analysis would have made him better disposed to the modern dissolution of quanta into vibrations, as would his acceptance of primordial matter make more readily acceptable its evolution. . . . Plato accepted an immanent divine principle that teleologically directs all things towards their 'telos' or end, and this is the source of Whitehead's praise for Plato. But it is important also to remember that for Plato this was the lowest level of reality, and that what is most truly divine remains totally beyond change.

. . . .

Suffice it to note at this stage that Plato could never have accepted the way in which Whitehead develops this notion in relation to God. His suggestion is that we think of God as having what he calls a 'primordial' and 'consequent' nature. 'Analogously to all actual entities, the nature of God is dipolar . . . The consequent nature of God is conscious; and it is the realisation of the actual world in the unity of his nature . . . The primordial nature is conceptual, the consequent nature is the weaving of God's physical feelings upon the primordial concepts.' Not perhaps surprisingly this language has led some commentators to doubt whether the primordial nature is anything more than an abstract concept. Whether correct as an interpretation of Whitehead or not, it is certainly a defect that his followers have sought to rectify. Ogden does this in part by making the analogy of the world as God's body more explicit. 'God is by analogy a living and ever growing God . . . and is related to the universe of other beings somewhat as the human self is related to its body. And yet, just as surely implied, is that God is even in these respects the truly eminent or perfect reality, whose unsurpassability is a matter of principle, not simply of fact.' The primordial nature is thus clearly conceived of as taking initiatives, as well as in turn being affected by the world.

As for what led Process theologians to these conclusions apart from the alleged greater compatibility of its fundamental category with a scientific outlook, two major types of argument can I think be detected. What seems to have weighed most with Whitehead was what he called his 'reformed subjectivist principle', 'the denial of . . . any meaning not abstracted from the experiential meaning'. In other words, the claim is that no sense can be attached to an account of God that is not based on that alone of which we have knowledge, namely our own experience. He informs us that 'consciousness presupposes experience, and not experience consciousness,' and applies this as much to God as to all physical reality. Hartshorne in similar vein argues that God cannot be described as personal unless like us he is capable of change in response to his environment, as also that he cannot properly be said to love unless his experience is like ours in being pained by others' sufferings and enriched by their achievements. If the first argument is conceptual, the second is primarily pragmatic. It is that if Christianity is to make an adequate response to secularism and restore something of the involved God of the Bible, then he must be located where men's real concerns are, i.e. in the world. This is an argument particularly popular with Ogden. Of traditional theism he remarks that 'the difficulty with the old theism's dymythologizing is that it does not really interpret the scriptural myths, but rather eliminates them.' His point is that classical analyses like that of Aquinas make the meaning of God's acts lie in what happens to men and not what happens to God.

Kenneth Surin, 'Process Theology', in David F. Ford (ed.), *The Modern Theologians: An Introduction to Christian Theology in the Twentieth Century*, II, Oxford, Blackwell, 1989, pp. 103–6

'Process theology' designates more than one theological movement or school. Most of its adherents are based in the United States, where it has taken three main directions, all of which have as their starting-point the metaphysical system adumbrated by Alfred North Whitehead. The philosophico-theological movements or tendencies constitutive of process theology came to real prominence in the 1960s.

. . . .

Alfred North Whitehead (1861–1947) was a logician, a metaphysician and a philosopher of science. He was not a theologian. But he did have an abiding interest in religion, and he made proposals which have profound implications for those interested in the availability of a 'philosophically' adequate doctrine of God.

Whitehead saw all 'actual entities' or 'actual occasions' (his terms) as being, in some measure, self-creative. God, however, is the eminent or unsurpassably superior form of self-creation. Whitehead harnesses to this principle the insight that a self-creative being must in some way be creative of divine reality. God is conscious of all entities, and since each entity manifests in an inferior way the self-creativity which God manifests supremely, all entities are co-creators of the divine reality. At least, they are creative of that aspect of divinity which is consequent upon the world. (This, 'Consequent Nature' of God is distinguished by Whitehead from the 'abstract' or 'Primordial Nature' of the divinity. It should also be noted that for Whitehead God is an 'actual entity', but since he is a nontemporal being, God is not an 'actual occasion'.) It is a corollary of these White-headian principles that every finite entity is essentially God-related, that God is the presupposition of the world, and the world the presupposition of God. A properly-constituted philosophical theology would therefore be one which sought to understand God in terms of the self-same concep-tuality by which all other entities are understood. It would in no way make God an exception to this conceptuality. These insights are given succinct expression by Whitehead in a famous series of antitheses:

It is as true to say that God is permanent and the World fluent, as that the World is permanent and God is fluent.

It is as true to say that God is one and the World many, as that the World is one and God many.

It is as true to say that, in comparison with the world, God is actual eminently, as that, in comparison with God, the World is actual eminently.

It is as true to say that the World is immanent in God, as that God is immanent in the World.

It is as true to say that God transcends the World, as that the world transcends God.

It is as true to say that God creates the World, as that the World creates God. (Whitehead, *Process and Reality*, 1929, p. 528)

The theistic metaphysics which ensues in these antitheses is used by process theologians to underpin what they regard as a new and philosophically adequate doctrine of God.

At the heart of process theology (in all its strands), therefore, is an attempt to dispense with, or at least to reconstruct, what its adherents take to be the God of 'classical theism'. This critique is usually accom-panied by the formulation of an alternative theism. Process theology thus accords a decisive centrality to the doctrine of God.

The divinity of process theism is a synthesis of concrete and abstract aspects: the latter comprising God's 'abstract' or 'necessary' attributes (the 'Primordial Nature' of deity, in Whitehead's terminology); the former God's 'concrete' or 'accidental' attributes (the 'Consequent Nature' of deity, in Whitehead's words). Its proponents hold neo-classical theism to part company with its classical counterpart precisely by virtue of its ascription to God of 'accidental' attributes – such attributes, it is held, cannot in principle be ascribed to God by orthodox Christian theism. Classical or 'monopolar' theism thus holds God to be devoid of relativity and becoming, whereas process or 'dipolar' theism predicates of God a supreme relativity and becoming (in respect of the 'concrete' pole of deity), *as well as* the attributes of eternity, absoluteness, necessity and independence (these being assigned to the 'abstract' pole of deity). Again, it is possible to use a set of antitheses – necessarily selective in this case – to indicate the nature of the relation between these two modes of deity:

ABSTRACT POLE	CONCRETE POLE
conceptual	objectual
objective	subjective
potential	actual
universal	particular
existent	actual
essential	accidental

These essentially complementary poles represent *dual* aspects of the *one* deity. Classical theism is said to be riven with contradictions precisely because it cannot countenance a 'dipolar' conception of deity. Several such contradictions are alleged to bedevil orthodox or 'monopolar' theism. Thus process theists charge that orthodox theists want to affirm that everything in God is necessary, including the divine will, although the world willed by God is contingent. Orthodox theists are also accused of maintaining that God knows and loves the creaturely realm, while denying that God is affected by that which is known and loved in this unsurpassable divine way. Again, orthodox theists are said to uphold an absolute divine omnipotence, which gives God an unqualified monopoly over all power. But if this is so, say process theists, how can creatures be said to have a real freedom which they can use or abuse? Classical theism is vitiated by such contradictions because it makes the mistake of thinking that the divine perfection entails a corresponding absoluteness. This assumption, however, is untenable. On the contrary, the more perfect something is, the more intimately it is related to other entities. Likewise, the more perfect a being is, the more it can be expected to register and to be impressed by the changes which take place in other beings. God is enriched and changed by the world. But God in turn changes and enriches the world by perfecting and passing back to it the actuality which had transformed his consequent nature. God perfects the world, and while the world changes God, it can never hope to surpass God in perfection. God alone is infinite. Process theism, therefore, is not a 'pantheism' but a *'panentheism'*: it asserts that God 'includes' the world but does not go on to say that the divine reality is reducible to the reality of the universe (if process theism made this reduction it would indeed be a pantheism).

David Basinger, *Divine Power in Process Theism: A Philosophical Critique,* **New York, State University of New York Press, 1988, pp. 2–4**

Our discussion will be limited to that variant of process theology which traces its basic metaphysical origins to the work of Whitehead and much of its explicitly theological framework to the interpretation of Whitehead offered by Charles Hartshorne. This Whiteheadian/Hartshornean tradition was initially championed by such individuals as Henry Nelson Wieman, Bernard Loomer and Daniel Day Williams. More recently, its best known proponents are John Cobb, Norman Pittenger, Schubert Ogden, Lewis Ford and David Griffin. I have chosen to concentrate my efforts on this tradition because I believe it to be the dominant school of process theological thought today and because I agree with those who argue that this tradition, more than any other process variant, has 'generated increasing interest and excitement as a philosophical basis for Christian thought'.

There is, not surprisingly, much significant diversity even within this camp. However, with the exception of one significant aspect of Odgen's system, the basic metaphysical tenets of this school of thought can be summarized as follows.

The most basic constituents of reality are not 'things' or enduring substances. Rather, they are little droplets of experience – usually called actual entities, actual occasions or energy-events – which momentarily come into existence and then immediately perish. Each of these actual entities has a 'physical' and 'mental' component. As the entity comes into existence, the 'physical' component takes account of (prehends) two things: its past – all that has gone before it – and God's initial aim – that which God sees as the best possibility open to it, given its concrete situation. It also automatically feels some impulse to act in accordance with God's leading. However, each entity has at least some power of self-determination – the function of its 'mental' components. Thus, no entity is ever forced to do what God wants. It always has the power to choose its own subjective aim from among God's initial aim and all other real possibilities its past has made available. Once this decision is made – once the entity has unified the data from its perspective – it perishes as an experiencing subject and its experience becomes an objective part of the past for all subsequent actual entities.

Some sets of entities, however, have a unity of their own. In these societies or aggregates of entities, each entity still inherits its past from all other entities. But its inheritance from the past members of its own society is dominant. A subatomic particle such as an electron is a good example of a basic, lower-level entity of this sort. There is no enduring substance that can be identified as an electron. But there are societies of serially-ordered 'electron' entities in which each occasion largely repeats the form of the previous entity in its society. In fact, the carry-over is so great that any given electron society appears to behave as if it were a single entity. Thus, such societies or aggregates are often called *enduring individuals.*

Moreover, basic serially-ordered enduring societies of a given type normally aggregate into more complexly structured societies (enduring individuals). Societies of subatomic particles form enduring atomic individuals which, themselves, aggregate with other enduring atomic individuals to form enduring molecular individuals which in turn aggregate with other molecular individuals. In the higher-order animal realm, for example, various societies of enduring cellular individuals aggregate to form enduring multicellular animal bodies with a central nervous system. And in some such enduring individuals, the enduring nervous system gives rise to what we label as the enduring human mind or soul.

In short, in process thought, the whole is truly greater than the sum of its parts. What we perceive phenomenologically as enduring individuals – for example, humans, dogs, cats, and trees – are not just bits of inanimate and animate matter in a certain configuration. Such enduring individuals are really 'societies of societies' of varying complexity, with each society retaining to some extent its own autonomous power of self-determination even as it combines with other societies of its type to create more complex societies (individuals).

However, the more complex societies in any given 'society of societies' are dominant. The enduring society we identify as the 'brain', for example, is normally dominant over the enduring societies we identify as the muscles, which in turn are dominant over the enduring societies of cells of which they are composed. This explains why enduring individuals such as dogs and humans normally appear to function as unified wholes.

Moreover, the more complex an enduring individual, the greater the influence of its 'mental' pole – that is, the more actual options it has open to it and the more conscious it is of such options. This explains why humans behave in much more creative, unpredictable ways than do dogs, which in turn behave in much more novel ways than do rocks.

Within process thought God is not exempted from this metaphysical order. Rather, God is considered the chief exemplification of it. God, like all other enduring individuals, is an actual entity – the supreme actual entity. And, like all other actual entities, God is dipolar. God's consequent nature – analogous to the 'physical' pole in other entities – takes account of (prehends) all that happens in the world [*prehension is Whitehead's term for a form of universal non-sensory perception and relation*]. Other actual entities are also 'aware' to some extent of all that has occurred. But God alone experiences in its fullness all that every other entity experiences. This means that although each actual entity exists only momentarily and no other actual entity experiences at any time the past in its entirety, the past is not lost. All past occasions exist eternally as a unified whole in God's consciousness. It is in this sense that God's being includes and penetrates the whole universe. Or, as Hartshorne puts it, it is in this sense that the world is God's body.

God, however, also has a primordial nature – analogous to the 'mental' pole in other entities – which responds to that which God experiences. God, in this capacity, is aware of all harmonized possibilities open to the world. And given this knowledge and the knowledge of each actual entity's individual past, God continuously presents to every entity at every moment the optimum real possibilities open to it. Moreover, as was mentioned before, each actual entity feels some compulsion (lure) to act in accordance with God's will, although such persuasion never overwhelms the entity's freedom to choose otherwise.

Thus it is that, while God is not exempted from the metaphysical rules which order the process system, God is certainly thought to be the most significant individual within it. Most process theists deny that God in any sense created the process. But all maintain that it is God alone who unifies this ontological process into a harmonized whole and that God certainly does exercise more influence on the direction of the process than does any other enduring individual.

2.2 The metaphysics of God

Schubert M. Ogden, *The Reality of God and Other Essays*, San Francisco, Harper & Row, 1977, pp. 56–61

Among the most significant intellectual achievements of the twentieth century has been the creation at last of a neo-classical alternative to the metaphysics and philosophical theology of our classical tradition. Especially through the work of Alfred North Whitehead and, in the area usually designated 'natural theology,' of Charles Hartshorne, the ancient problems of philosophy have received a new, thoroughly modern treatment, which in its scope and depth easily rivals the so-called *philosophia perennis* [*'the perennial philosophy': the supposed common strand of wisdom within all the great religions*]. It is my belief that the conceptuality provided by this new philosophy enables us so to conceive the reality of God that we may respect all that is legitimate in modern secularity, while also fully respecting the distinctive claims of Christian faith itself. In the rest of the essay, I shall try to give the reasons for this belief.

The starting-point for a genuinely new theistic conception is what Whitehead speaks of as 'the reformed subjectivist principle'. According to this principle, we can give an adequate answer to the metaphysical question of the meaning of 'reality' only by imaginatively generalizing 'elements disclosed in the analysis of the experiences of subjects'. In other words, the principle requires that we take as the experiential basis of all our most fundamental concepts the primal phenomenon of our own existence as experiencing subjects or selves.

To adhere to this requirement is to be led ineluctably to a distinctly different kind of metaphysics and philosophical theology from those of the classical tradition. As not only Whitehead, but also Heidegger and others have made clear, the characteristics of classical philosophy all derive from its virtually exclusive orientation away from the primal phenomenon of selfhood toward the secondary phenomenon of the world constituted by the experience of our senses. It assumes that the paradigmatic cases of reality are the objects of ordinary perception – such things as tables and chairs, and persons as we may know them by observing their behavior – and from these objects it constructs its fundamental concepts or categories of interpretation. The chief of these categories is that of 'substance' or 'being,' understood as that which is essentially nontemporal and lacking in real internal relations to anything beyond itself. Insofar as the self is focused by classical philosophy, it, too, is interpreted in these categories and thus conceived as a special kind of substance. As soon, however, as we orient our metaphysical reflection to the self as we actually experience it, as itself the primal ground of our world of perceived objects, this whole classical approach is, in the Heideggerian sense of the word, 'dismantled' (*destruiert*). Whatever else the self is, it is hardly a substance which, in Descartes' phrase, 'requires nothing but itself in order to exist,' nor is it altogether without intrinsic temporal structure. To the contrary, the very being of the self is relational or social; and it is nothing if not a process of change involving the distinct modes of present, past and future.

To exist as a self, as each of us does, is always to be related, first of all, to the intimate world constituted by one's own body. What I think and feel has its most direct effects on my own brain cells and central nervous system, and thence on the rest of the organism in which I as a self am incarnate. Likewise, what most directly affects me as a conscious subject is just the incredibly complex state of that same organism in which I as a self participate by immediate sympathetic feeling. By means of my body, then, I am also affected by, and in turn affect, the larger whole of things beyond myself. But, whether directly or indirectly, I am really related to an encompassing society of other beings and am a self at all only by reason of that real relatedness. No less constitutive of my self-hood is its essential temporality. I know myself most immediately only as an ever-changing sequence of occasions of experience, each of which is the present integration of remembered past and anticipated future into a new whole of significance. My life history continually leads through moments of decision in which I must somehow determine what both I and those with whom I am related are to be. Selecting from the heritage of the already actual and the wealth of possibility awaiting realization, I freely fashion myself in creative interaction with a universe of others who also are not dead but alive.

If we begin by taking the self as thus experienced as paradigmatic for reality as such, the result is a complete revolution of classical metaphysics. It thereupon becomes clear that real internal relation to others and intrinsic temporality are not 'mixed perfections' peculiar to finite beings such as ourselves, but 'simple perfections' inherent in the meaning of 'reality' in the most fundamental use of the word. In consequence, the chief category for finally interpreting anything real can no longer be 'substance' or 'being' (as traditionally understood), but must be 'process' or 'creative becoming' construed as that which is in principle social and temporal. Whatever is, is to be conceived, in the last analysis, either as an instance of, or an element in, such creative becoming and thus as somehow analogous to our own existence as selves.

By *this* 'analogy of being,' however, God, too, must be conceived as a genuinely temporal and social reality, and therefore as radically different from the wholly timeless and unrelated Absolute of traditional theism [*the 'analogy of being' is the relation of similarity between created and uncreated being*]. This is not to say that God is to be thought of as only one more instance of creative becoming alongside all the others. As we saw earlier, the idea of God cannot be thought at all unless that to which it refers is in all ways truly supreme, a unique reality qualitatively different from everything else. But this may all be granted, indeed, insisted upon, even though one still maintains that God must be conceived in strict analogy with ourselves. The whole point of any *analogia entis* is to enable one to think and speak of God in meaningful concepts, while yet acknowledging that those concepts apply to him only in an eminent sense, which is in principle different from that intended in their other uses. All that a valid method of analogy requires is that the eminence attributed to God really follow from, rather than contradict, the positive meaning of our fundamental concepts as given them by experience. Just this, of course, . . . the classical practice of analogy is unable to do. Because it rests on the premise that God can be in no sense really relative or temporal, it can say that he 'knows' or 'loves' only by contradicting the meaning of those words as we otherwise use them.

On neo-classical premises, this difficulty, along with innumerable others, is at last removed. God is now conceived as precisely the unique or in all ways perfect instance of creative becoming, and so as the one reality which is eminently social and temporal. Instead of being merely the barren Absolute, which by definition can be really related to nothing, God is in truth related to everything, and that through an immediate sympathetic participation of which our own relation to our bodies is but an image. Similarly, God is no longer thought of as utterly unchangeable and empty of all temporal distinctions. Rather, he, too, is understood to be continually in process of self-creation, synthesizing in each new moment of his experience the whole of achieved actuality with the plenitude of possibility as yet unrealized.

This implies, naturally, that God is by analogy a living and even growing God and that he is related to the universe of other beings somewhat as the human self is related to its body. And yet, just as surely implied is that God is even in these respects the truly eminent or perfect reality, whose unsurpassability by others is a matter of principle, not simply of fact. If God is the *eminently* temporal and changing One, to whose time and change there can be neither beginning nor end, then he must be just as surely the One who is also eternal and unchangeable. *That* he is everchanging is itself the product or effect of no change whatever, but is in the strictest sense changeless, the immutable ground of change as such, both his own and all others. Likewise, the notion that God is not utterly immaterial or bodiless ('without body, parts, or passions'), but, on the contrary, is the *eminently* incarnate One establishes a qualitative difference between his being and everything else. The human self, as we noted, is incarnate in the world only in a radically inferior fashion. It directly interacts with little more than its own brain cells, and so is always a localized self, limited by an encompassing external environment. As the eminent Self, by radical contrast, God's sphere of interaction or body is the whole universe of nondivine beings, with each one of which his relation is unsurpassably immediate and direct. His only environment is wholly internal, which means that he can never be localized in any particular space and time but is omnipresent. Hence, just because God is the *eminently* relative One, there is also a sense in which he is strictly absolute. His being related to all others is itself relative to nothing, but is the absolute ground of any and all real relationships, whether his own or those of his creatures.

In its way, therefore, a neo-classical conception of God's reality incorporates all the 'metaphysical attributes' on which classical theists alone insist. For it, too, God is in a literal sense 'eternal,' 'immutable,' 'impassive,' 'immaterial' – in brief, the metaphysical Absolute. The difference, however – and it is radical – is that God is now conceived not as simply identical with the Absolute, but as the supremely relative Self or Thou who includes the Absolute as the abstract principle of his own concrete identity. In other words, the traditional attributes of God are all reconceived on the analogical basis provided by our own existence as selves. Just as in our case, our defining characteristics are but abstract elements in our concrete experiences, so in the case of God, his attributes are really only abstractions. As such, they define that sense of his eminence or perfection which is indeed statically complete, an absolute maximum. But, because they are in themselves nothing more than abstractions, they are far from constituting the whole of his perfection. That, to the contrary, is nothing merely abstract, but something unimaginably concrete: the ever new synthesis into his own everlasting and all-embracing life of all that has been or ever shall be.

Such, in its main outlines, is the new theism I am proposing.

John B. Cobb, Jr., *A Christian Natural Theology: Based on the Thought of Alfred North Whitehead,* **London, Lutterworth, 1965, pp. 161–4, 166–7, 178, 203–6**

The discussion has thus far focused upon what Whitehead calls the primordial nature of God. This is God as the principle of limitation and the organ of novelty who achieves these ends by his ordered envisagement of the realm of eternal objects. This is the only way God was conceived in *Science and the Modern World*. It is the primary emphasis in *Religion in the Making* and in the first 522 pages of *Process and Reality*. However, in *Religion in the Making* and in scattered passages in *Process and Reality* there is another theme. Alongside the description of God as the primordial actual entity are passages about the effect of the temporal occasions upon God. For example, in *Religion in the Making*, Whitehead described God as 'the ideal companion who transmutes what has been lost into a living fact within his own nature'. Now in the closing pages of *Process and Reality*, Whitehead returns to this theme of what he now calls the consequent nature of God.

In the discussion of the primordial nature of God, even though Whitehead sees importance for religion, philosophical considerations alone are relevant. The survey of religious experience in *Religion in the Making* serves chiefly to reinforce the philosophical conclusions. In the discussion of the consequent nature, on the other hand, it is clear that philosophical and religious concerns are interrelated in Whitehead's presentation. Here, however, we will focus on the philosophical.

The consequent nature of God is God's physical pole, his prehension of the actual occasions constituting the temporal world. Since these occasions come to be successively, there is successiveness in the divine nature that suggests temporality. However, the perpetual perishing that constitutes the temporality of the world is absent to God. Hence, God in his consequent nature is called everlasting.

God's prehension of the temporal occasions objectifies them with a completeness necessarily lacking in such prehensions within the temporal world. Furthermore, since there is no perishing in God, that completeness remains forever. This means that every achievement of value in the temporal world is preserved everlastingly in God's consequent nature. This sense of the preservation of values in God's memory was of great religious importance to Whitehead. Partly for this reason, some of his expressions of this preservation seem to suggest an element that the philosophical position in general does not clearly imply. That element is the living immediacy of the occasions as preserved in God. The more normal assumption would be that just as in temporal experience only that which is past is prehended, so also in God's experience temporal occasions are prehended only as they perish. They could no longer enjoy subjective immediacy. It is reasonable to suppose that God's prehension would be far more inclusive of the elements in the satisfaction of the prehended occasions, but the subjective immediacy of the occasion is not one of those elements.

. . .

Another important feature of God's consequent nature is that it is conscious. Whitehead does not explain this, but from his general discussion of consciousness the reason can readily be learned. God in his primordial nature alone has no consciousness because this nature consists in purely conceptual feelings, and such feelings are never conscious. Consciousness requires the interweaving of the physical feelings with conceptual feelings. This involves God's prehension of the world, his consequent nature.

A final feature of the consequent nature of God is barely treated in the last two paragraphs of the book. Like most of the rest of the ideas about God in *Process and Reality*, it was foreshadowed in *Religion in the Making*. It is demanded by the principle of universal relativity that just as God in his consequent nature prehends us, so also we prehend God's consequent nature.

. . .

I have written, and Whitehead sometimes writes, as though there were no philosophical reason for affirming the consequent nature of God other than the demand of a coherent completion of the idea of God as actual entity. This is not quite true. There are two points in *Process and Reality* at which he seems to give independent philosophical arguments for the existence of the consequent nature of God. The two arguments are closely related in character, and both affirm the need that there be a perspective in which what is sheer multiplicity from any temporal point of view has unity. In the first instance, Whitehead is discussing the claim of his own thought to approximate to truth. What can this mean? We all sense that there is some structure to which our formulations more or less adequately approximate. But if we are trying to speak of reality as a whole, where is this structure? Whitehead answers that it can only be in the consequent nature of God. Otherwise we would have only a multiplicity of finite and distorting perspectives that could afford no standard.

The second argument is more obscure. It runs like this. The initial data of a complex feeling constitute a single nexus that has a pattern. But this pattern is not prehended by the members of the nexus. Is the pattern then imposed upon the nexus by the prehending occasion? Whitehead thinks not. When we perceive a pattern, we perceive something that is given to us, not something we create. But if it is given to us and is not in the data prehended, it can only be in the consequent nature of God.

A third argument can be derived from Whitehead's thought by implication. The evidence for it is less clearly found in *Process and Reality* than in *Religion in the Making*, yet it seems to be present in the philosophy of Whitehead in such a way that this third argument is really more fundamental than the two just summarized. If God is understood to provide different initial aims to each occasion, and in each case just that aim that is ideally suited to it, then God seems, in the provision of the initial aim, to be taking account of the world in all its change. This effect of the world upon God is an essential part of the process whereby God functions as the principle of limitation.

Whatever weight we may attach to these arguments, Whitehead's own thought placed the burden of the argument for God's existence upon the necessity of a principle of limitation. Further, he associated this principle with the primordial nature of God. Hence in his presentation, the consequent nature of God appears more as a speculative extension of the doctrine than as an essential part.

. . .

The objection to Whitehead's formulation . . . is that too often he deals with the two natures as though they were genuinely separable. Further, he frequently writes as though God were simply the addition of these two natures. Thus God's primordial nature performs certain functions and his consequent nature others. But according to Whitehead's own understanding, this cannot be the precise and adequate formulation. Actual entities are unities composed of a synthesis of their mental and physical poles, but they are not exhaustively analyzable into these two poles. In such analysis we would omit precisely the subjective unity, the concrete satisfaction, the power of decision and self-creation. It is always the actual entity that acts, not one of its poles as such, although in many of its functions one pole or another may be primarily relevant. Whitehead must certainly have meant to say this also about God, but his separate and contrasting treatment of the two natures is misleading – indeed, I believe that he was himself misled into exaggerating their separability.

. . .

In Whitehead's analysis, God's role in creation centers in the provision to each actual occasion of its initial aim. This role is of such importance that Whitehead on occasion acknowledges that God may properly be conceived in his philosophy as the creator of all temporal entities.

Yet, more frequently, he opposes the various connotations of the term 'creator', as applied to God, and prefers to speak of God and the temporal world as jointly qualifying or conditioning creativity, which then seems to play the ultimate role in creation.

. . .

Whitehead does restrict the creative role of God in such a way that his sole responsibility for what happens is effectively and properly denied.

First, the initial aim is the aim that is ideal for that occasion *given its situation*. It is not God's ideal for the situation in some abstract sense. It is the adaptation of God's purposes to the actual world. Second, the initial aim does not determine the outcome, although it profoundly influences it. In subsequent phases the occasion adjusts its aim and makes its own decision as to the outcome it will elicit from the situation given to it. The actual occasion is its own creator, *causa sui*, Whitehead likes to say. In the third place, God does not create the eternal objects. He presupposes them just as they, for their efficacy in the world, presuppose him. In the fourth place, Whitehead envisions no beginning of the world, hence no first temporal creation out of nothing. In every moment there is given to God a world that has in part determined its own form and that is free to reject in part the new possibilities of ideal realization he offers it. This is certainly a different understanding of God as creator from that which has been customary in many Christian circles, but it is nevertheless a doctrine of God as creator.

2.3 Tensions and criticisms

Colin E. Gunton, *Becoming and Being: The Doctrine of God in Charles Hartshorne and Karl Barth*, Oxford, Oxford University Press, 1978, pp. 19–23

The criticisms of the tradition from the point of view of logic and the movement of thought would nearly all seem to have been well made. . . . Basically they depend on the very reasonable point that if God is totally unrelated to the world, and, like the Epicurean gods, is totally unaffected by its suffering, the value of the created order is called in question, at least from the point of view of God.

First it is argued that if the reality of God remains unchanged whatever we do, there is really very little point in performing one act rather than another. Because 'traditional theism posits among the circumstances of all acts the existence of an absolutely perfect being', it would appear to follow 'that no act can, in its consequences, be better than any other', for the same unchanging reality remains in either case. Here Hartshorne alludes to the conception of God's perfection, . . . as the sum total of reality, and would appear to make the point that, *sub specie aeternitatis*, as it were, no act of a finite being can make the slightest difference to the over-all state of affairs.

But, second, there are other charges to be laid than that of encouraging men to believe that ethical choice is of no ultimate importance. It has in fact encouraged them to regard themselves as something ultimate. If, it is argued, men's worship of God does not affect God, it can only be self-regarding. But man can never be something ultimate. While this particular charge may appear to be rather far-fetched, there may be more substance in the related point that the notion of a self-sufficient God has tended to promote the cultivation of self-sufficiency in men as an ethical ideal and 'the dangerous individualism of our Western world'. Further, it is claimed, the idea of providence that has developed on the soil of classical theism 'has sometimes encouraged extreme conservatism . . . and sometimes doctrinaire progressivism . . .'

Moreover, the cultural origins of this concept of God are not wholly respectable in the modern world, and reveal a relationship between God and man that is morally repugnant. The concept of a totally independent deity 'seems plainly an idealisation of the tyrant-subject relationship . . .' Not only is it morally repugnant, but it contradicts basic insights of the Christian faith. 'How can anyone believe that being a follower of Jesus is like being an imitator of Aristotle's divine Aristocrat, who is serenely indifferent to the world's turmoil?' If a defence is attempted along the lines of Anselm's that God is only compassionate in terms of our experience, but not of his, that 'is to mock us'. Real compassion would seem to require genuine relation and even suffering. Otherwise, it is difficult to see how the compassion is anything but an act, a hollow sham.

The *cantus firmus* beneath all these points in Hartshorne's genuine and serious concern that the things men do and the choices they make should matter, particularly in the sense that they should make some real difference to the way things are. They should not merely be acts in some play that has been written from eternity, 'a single absolute world-plan, complete in every detail from eternity, and executed with inexorable power'. What makes the situation worse is that there is no need to subscribe to the classical concept. As a matter of fact men have usually, throughout the history of religion, preferred what Hartshorne calls a dipolar conception of God. . . . Broadly speaking, what he means is that God is conceived to be such that in part of his being he is affected by the doings of other entities, and in particular that he is able to suffer with them, while in the other part he is such that his very existence cannot be threatened by what he suffers. He is indeed fully God in the security of his position in the universe, but this does not prevent him from participating in the lives of his creatures. The error of the classical theists is that in their concern for his godness, they stressed only one pole of the divine reality – their doctrine was *monopolar* – with the result that they neglected important aspects of what mankind has instinctively felt God to be.

If we examine the history of religion, and forget the dogmas on which traditional theism has been based, we shall see that the worshipper has in fact considered God to be dipolar rather than monopolar. Take, for example, the ancient religious thinkers who failed to conceptualize their beliefs philosophically, but whose understanding of God is distorted if it is forced into the classical mould. These early theists are represented by, among others, the pharaoh Ikhnaton, with his 'poetic outpourings', the biblical writers, and Plato. There are dipolar elements in them all, and Plato is held to be particularly important because in the final dialogues 'both categories – absolute fixity and absolute mobility – find expression'. But, more important from the point of view of this study, we should note Hartshorne's judgement on the biblical writings. Far from affirming a monopolar God, 'they often seem to imply a dipolar conception'. But they are essentially naïve in what they affirm and must, we might say, be demythologized. For Hartshorne, and in this respect he has far more in common with the classical theologians than with Karl Barth, 'meta-phorical expressions like "the wrath of God" or his "pity" ' may be charac-terized as 'wholly non-literal concessions to the weakness of the human understanding; still, it may be suggested that the minimum to be expressed by such metaphors is this: that God is not blankly neutral to the happenings in the world . . .' God could not be supposed literally to love, pity, or be angry. The philosopher knows better. His very function is to provide a superior representation of the divine reality to the anthro-pomorphic, mythological representations of God in scripture. The error of the classical metaphysicians lies not in their undertaking a programme, but in their making a mess of it by their neglect of the second pole of the divine reality. Hartshorne believes that there is a test by which we can see the failure of their project. There should be a two-way relation between the 'religious' or uninterpreted ideas and the secular concepts employed by the philosopher. In the case of the classical concept this is not so. While it may be possible to derive the religious tenets from the non-religious – though this is only possible 'after a fashion' – the reverse is not possible.

In other words, It is not the function of the metaphysical theologian to force the intuitions of the worshipper into a procrustean bed of abstract ideas that have already been established *a priori;* rather, it is his job to purify the crude expressions of religion in such a way that there is a two-way logical relationship between the two sets of terms. The philosopher must reflect accurately, and indeed with a precision the original lacks, the beliefs of the ordinary religious person. Hartshorne thinks he has achieved this. In the dipolar doctrine of God 'the "personal" conception

of deity required in religion is reconciled with the requirements of philo-
sophic reason'. In fact 'It is a belief of many today that the "new" theology
is more, not less, religious than the old, at least if religion means "devoted
love for a being regarded as superlatively worthy of love", which is the
Christian conception and to some extent the conception of the higher
religions generally.'

Thomas F. Tracy, *God, Action and Embodiment*, Grand Rapids, Michigan, Eerdmans, 1984, pp. 112–15

Suppose, then, that we think of God and world as a single, indissolubly
unified, though unimaginably complex psychophysical agent. What will
be required if we are to develop this view? The first point to note is that
we must draw as close a parallel as possible between the universe (all
that is) and a living organism. It will not do to portray the universe simply
as an aggregate of many individuals that may interact with each other but
that do not combine in any overall harmonious function. Rather we must
see the universe as an organic whole the many constituents of which are
integrated in a single operative unity. This will be a point of particular
vulnerability for this theological proposal. Clearly, the project of conceiving of God as a psychophysical agent will be threatened if this picture of
the totality of things is seriously called in question. It would be very difficult, however, to say how far one might back away from these claims
about the organic unity of the universe and still have a viable basis for talk
of God and world as a psychophysical unity. That is a debate I will not try
to conduct here.

   If we can successfully construe our world as a single, functionally unified individual, then we may speak of God as the agent whose life is
grounded in and constituted by the cosmic organism. Given a non-
dualist understanding of the bodily agent as a psychophysical unit, God
cannot be said to exist as a distinct being apart from and over against the
world. Just as the human agent is not to be identified with an immaterial
substance that controls the body, so God is not to be thought of as a
supernatural power who intervenes 'from above' to act upon the physical
world. If we refuse to picture the human agent as a 'ghost in the
machine,' then we should no longer represent God as a 'ghost in the
universe'. To say that the world is God's body is to say that the processes
unfolding in the universe are the processes of God's life, that God does
not exist except in and through these processes.

   On the other hand, God will not be identified with the physical universe
in any sense that precludes his being the bearer of a distinctive personal

identity as an agent. It will not be enough to say simply that God *is* the organically unified system of activity that constitutes the totality of things, for as I have already argued, an organic system of activity (i.e., a body) is not an agent unless it operates intentionally in at least a small range of its activities. As the agent whose life is the world process, God is not to be located outside that process; his actions are events within the universe, and not events that break in upon the universe. But God's actions are not merely the occurrence of certain processes in the physical universe; rather, they are the *enactment* of those processes for the achievement of his purposes. Just as human agents possess a capacity to intentionally vary certain of the processes that constitute bodily life, so God can intentionally regulate at least some of the processes that constitute the universe as an organic totality.

God is, in this sense, creative. His activity as agent organizes the various processes at work in the universe into patterns expressive of his purpose for the overall achievement of the 'world process'. His capacity for intentional action may extend far down into the stable patterns that lie at the foundation of his activity as well. If so, his capacity to realize his intentions for the 'life' of the universe (which is his life) will be vastly greater than the power we exercise over the formation of our lives. The divine agent, that is, will be profoundly self-creative. In addition, the divine agent may be eminently self-conscious. His awareness of the individual constituents that are functionally interrelated in the cosmic organism will be vastly more detailed and sympathetic than any human self-knowledge or interpersonal understanding. Given this concern for the constituents that are united in his life, God's intentional activity will be eminently well-considered, maximizing the realization of preferred possibilities in any situation and minimizing the sacrifice of positive values. God will be continuously at work throughout the whole range of his intentional capacities, bringing into actuality all of the highest possibilities contained in any moment of world process.

But while God is an eminently creative agent, he cannot be said to be the creator of the universe in any traditional theological sense. God may shape, direct, and organize the world process to a degree that far exceeds the limited self-creativity we exercise in our own lives, but he does not bring the universe into being or sustain it in its existence (though he may preserve certain of the patterns of cosmic process that he purposefully enacts). Since the 'life' of the cosmos is the life of God, God cannot be said to bring the cosmos into being without implying that he brings himself into being. Not even the boldest enthusiast for paradox, however, is likely to embrace the claim that God creates himself *ex nihilo*.

Furthermore, if God is to be bodily in both of the respects in which human beings are bodily, then his creative activity must finally be rooted in a pattern of life immune to intentional variation. God's powers of action may be of vastly greater scope and significance than ours, but they will nonetheless be finite. Though God is eminently self-creative, he is not unconditionally so. God's creative will is limited to possibilities established by the subintentional processes in which his life is grounded. In this respect, God's creativity is directly parallel to our own. The divine agent works with what is given for him, and must do the best he can with it. God does not freely commit himself to an intimate and vulnerable association with the world's process: he *is* that process. God's life is not complete apart from the life of the world, any more than the human agent's life is complete apart from bodily life. In the full expression of the positive possibilities of the world process lies the fulfillment of God's own existence. The unfolding world process will be the process of God's own self-realization.

There is a great deal more that might be said in developing this account of God as a psychophysical agent, but enough has been said here to indicate the key structures of this type of proposal. We need to note briefly some of its vulnerabilities. There are, of course, difficulties with the central analogies upon which the proposal trades. I pointed out initially that one may question whether 'the totality of things' can plausibly be construed as a functionally unified organism. There is a complementary problem that must also be mentioned. If the universe is construed as a cosmic organism, it appears that its unity will be too close to allow for the integrity of creatures as independent centers of activity interacting with God – that is, not only does our world appear to be too loose an association of individuals to pass as a cosmic organism, but a living body appears to require too tight a unity to permit the emergence of its constituents as agents in their own right. If one stresses the organic unity of creatures as the body of God, one threatens their standing as distinct individuals over against God. Yet if one stresses the interpersonal character of our relation to God, then one weakens the organismic unity of the world as a single individual.

Proponents of the organismic analogy have not been blind to these tensions. Charles Hartshorne, in what remains the most powerful development of this view, explicitly takes on the task of combining mind-body and interpersonal analogies in his account of the relation of God and world. In his early work Hartshorne develops a panpsychism that treats persons (both human and divine) as complex societies of lower order centers of activity. His case is strengthened by the evident correctness of the suggestion that a human life is a complex organization of many subordinate units of activity which are organized hierarchically in the overall structure of bodily life. If these subcenters of activity are to be agents, however, each must be allowed a unity of operation and a distinctness of intention that is sufficient to mark it out as a unique individual. Yet these unique individuals must also be so intimately interconnected that, as a whole, they constitute an irreducibly unified life. This 'super-individual' is not an additional entity conjoined to the many 'sub-individuals' (i.e, subordinate individuals) who are its constituents; rather, it *is* these many sub-individuals in their interrelatedness. The functional unit as a whole possesses a unique identity as a subject of experience and agent of intentional actions.

Puzzles abound at this point. Can a single event be an action in precisely the same sense for both the sub-individuals and the super-individual? If so, can they be distinct agents? Are the actions of sub-individuals to be understood as enactments of the super-individual's intentions? If so, are the sub-individuals agents in their own right at all? Is the action of the super-individual simply the accumulated effect of the actions of many sub-individuals? If so, is the super-individual an agent in any significant sense? Does the super-individual act by somehow influencing the actions of the many sub-individuals? If so, is the super-individual surreptitiously being treated as a distinct entity that acts upon the society of many sub-individuals? The effect of such questions is to apply pressure to each side of the social-individual hybrid that Hartshorne has produced. Despite the imaginative skill of Hartshorne's discussion, the central tension remains. It is not clear that a society of distinct agents can be so closely bound together as to take on the unity of a single organism. Nor is it clear that the constituents of a living organism can possess an independence of action sufficient to constitute a society of selves.

Colin E. Gunton, *Becoming and Being: The Doctrine of God in Charles Hartshorne and Karl Barth*, Oxford, Oxford University Press, 1978, pp. 220–4

Hartshorne's theology represents a version of the very ancient philosophical equation of reality and value. In his case the doctrine is that reality is getting better all the time because it is building upon the value of the past which accumulates in the divine memory. Neoclassical theology therefore asks us to take our view of reality from a general doctrine of becoming which is axiomatically optimistic. There is no doubt that in this respect there has to be a choice between the general and the particular becoming of God. We have seen that for Hartshorne christological considerations can be no more than symbolic of deeper truths that have already been decided philosophically. But this theological argument can be supported by a more general point. In his exposition of Barth's trinitarian theology Jüngel says, 'It is not . . . legitimate to confuse the statement, "God's being is in his becoming" with statements like, "God's being is becoming".' One reason for this can be seen in the light of the exposition of Hartshorne's concept of God. It is difficult to accept that the general becoming in which God's reality consists can properly be characterized as love. Merely because God is so constituted that everything that happens must make an impact upon him – a kind of metaphysical sponge, infinitely absorbent – are we to say that he *loves* everything? If we are going to use words like 'love' and 'grace' when we speak of God must there not be clear connotations of free, active, personal initiative if the existence of this God is going to make any more difference than serving as a validation for what man already is? The difficulty with the neoclassical suffering, for all its merits as a pointer to the real concern of God for his creatures, is that it is not also a doing. It is totally automatic and involuntary. It is not under God's control, for he has no choice as to whether or not he suffers with the world; in fact, he is under the control of the cosmic forces which make him what he is.

For the metaphysician, on the other hand, the trouble with Barth's radically personalistic conception will be that it is 'anthropomorphic', or 'mythological' to use the much misused modern cliché. Hartshorne is firmly anchored in that tradition of Western philosophy which regards philosophical abstractions as intellectually more respectable than the allegedly cruder anthropomorphisms of biblical origin. Of course, language has to be qualified when it is used of God and apart from its everyday use . . . But the weakness of neoclassical analogy is that its process of qualification so weakens the personal content of the terms that it virtually disappears. The cause of this is found in the metaphysical assumptions and methods of the system. If God can only be described by means of language that must also be predicable of all other reality, there is a danger – here amply illustrated – of philosophy being a search for a lowest common denominator. The outcome is twofold. On the one hand, such qualities as grace, mercy, and personality have in some sense to be ascribed to all entities before they can be attributed to God in an eminent sense. But, on the other, since what can be attributed to every entity is only personal in the most attenuated sense, the primary category of the philosophy is found to be something less than personal or rather a term sufficiently ambiguous to cover both the personal and the subpersonal, like 'relation'. The philosophy then becomes inevitably procrustean, the attenuation is carried upwards into the concept of God and there follow all the consequences that were set out in the first half of the study. Paradoxically, therefore, in view of the panpsychism of the doctrine, to ascribe personal qualities to God requires a straining of the metaphysical categories in theological special pleading. By appealing to such a metaphysical system as this in support of their theology, Christian theologians are likely to find the problems of demonstrating the meaningfulness of their doctrine compounded.

. . .

The theology that wishes to stand on the intellectual feet of a philosophy is likely to remain a cripple. Moreover, it demonstrates the lunacy of so much as taking seriously the rationalist dogma that philosophical abstractions are more intellectually appropriate than personal analogies when speaking of God. It makes clear the choice either that the Christian doctrine of the incarnation be relativized and shown to be no more than a pictorial ('mythological') expression of what the philosopher can say better – though, it must be noted, always with a very different meaning – or that the rationalist dogma be itself overcome by the Word's becoming flesh in Jesus of Nazareth.

The case for the rationalistic dogma becomes weaker when it is realized that in the case of neoclassical rationalism at least, the anthropomorphism remains unconquered by philosophical abstraction, even if it is spread thinly throughout the system. Hartshorne's theology is irretrievably anthropomorphic. 'God's "memory" is perfect; His "intentions" are unimpeachable; but does He *really* have "intentions", does He really have a will, does He really decide anything? "Memory" is no less anthropomorphic than "will"' (Julian Hartt). That brief sceptical comment sums up many of the internal and other weaknesses of Hartshorne's theology. Most of the problems arise when he tries to elevate universal relatedness, universal passivity, into love, in the hope that the transition from impersonal to personal, from metaphysical to anthropomorphic, will pass unnoticed. Whatever the value of the exposure of the contradictions and moral shortcomings of the classical concept of God, it is of little benefit to overthrow a tyrant if he is replaced by an ineffectual weakling, and that is the impression that remains whatever stress is laid upon the divine influence and persuasion.

This criticism could be put less metaphorically by pointing once more to the particular conception of suffering that dominates this theory of the divine relativity. The essential powerlessness of this deity derives from the way in which he is conceived to be related to the rest of reality, and this itself follows from the basic conception of perception with which this study began. Beings, whether God, man, or molecule perceive what is in their immediate past. Therefore, '. . . God cannot unify the world, since he can prehend the things in it only after their subjective reality or process has ceased to be.' Precisely so: because God 'happens' only after the entities he perceives have happened, they are the real creators of what there is. They it is who, though certainly under the influence of the God who is in their past, make the world to be what it really is. Process theology has been described as a sophisticated form of animism. It is therefore highly mythological, as its God is the projection into timeless truth of a certain conception of human experience. More than that, it represents a superstitious form of idolatry, in that it divinizes the world, both as the creator of itself and God and as the body, coeternal and consubstantial, of God who is its soul. If they had realized some of the implications of these doctrines, modern theologians would not perhaps have been quite so eager to employ this philosophy in defence of their faith. But then again, perhaps they would; for the ways of theological fashion in this century are as mysterious as the free choice exercised by Hartshorne's ultimate particles.

Topics for discussion

1 What features of classical theism is Process Theology reacting against? Are its advocates right to claim that process is the fundamental character of our world, or are more substantial claims still possible, for example, in respect of something called 'human nature' or our own personal identity?

2 How plausible is the 'reformed subjectivist principle' (i.e. that God must be like what we know in this world)? Should this be seen as a major restriction on God being a radically different kind of being from us, or as a simple application of the Christian doctrine that human beings are in the image of God? Or neither, but a basic point of epistemology, that we can only make deductions from what we already know?

3 Identify and explain some of the key terms employed by Process Theology. What is meant by God's 'antecedent nature'? Why have more recent writers sought to stress God's 'consequent nature' more strongly than Whitehead did? What is the relation between

these two terms and 'occasions'? How do 'occasions' come to constitute 'enduring individuals?' What is implied by talk of them having a 'mental' and 'physical pole'? What is it to 'prehend' an 'occasion'? Why can this only be done after 'the subjective reality' has ceased to exist?

4 Outline the principal advantages and disadvantages of speaking of the world as God's body. For instance, does the analogy help to present God as more responsive to, or interactive with, the world, or does it make his intentions problematic (and thus raise the question of whether he is truly personal)?

5 Is it fair of Gunton to accuse Process Theology of being fundamentally anthropomorphic and mythological? If so, should it be more properly characterized as a form of religious piety rather than an alternative metaphysic, as it claims? Or are these false alternatives?

3   God or Gaia?

The environmental challenge

3.1 Earthy spirituality

Thomas Berry, 'The Spirituality of the Earth', in Charles Birch, William Eakin and Jay B. McDaniel (eds), *Liberating Life: Contemporary Approaches to Ecological Theology*, Maryknoll, New York, Orbis, 1990, pp. 152–5

Creation in traditional Christian teaching is generally presented as part of the discussion concerning 'God in himself and in relation to his creation.' But creation in this metaphysical, biblical, medieval, theological context is not terribly helpful in understanding the creation process as set forth in the scientific manuals or the textbooks of the earth sciences as they are studied by children in elementary or high school, or later in college.

These classroom studies initiate the child into a world that has more continuity with later adult life in its functional aspect than does the catechetical story of creation taken from biblical sources. This schoolroom presentation of the world in which the child lives and finds a place in the world is all-important for the future spirituality of the child. The school fulfills in our times the role of the ancient initiation rituals, which introduced our children to the society and to their human and sacred role in this society. The tragedy is that the sacred or spiritual aspect of this process is now absent. It is doubtful if separate catechetical instructions with their heavy emphasis on redemptive processes can ever supply what is missing.

It may be that the later alienation of young adults from the redemptive tradition is, in some degree, due to this inability to communicate to the child a spirituality grounded more deeply in creation dynamics in accord with the modern way of experiencing the galactic emergence of the universe, the shaping of the earth, the appearance of life and of human consciousness, and the historical sequence in human development.

In this sequence the child might learn that the earth has its intrinsic spiritual quality from the beginning, for this aspect of the creation story is what has been missing. This is what needs to be established if we are to have a functional spirituality. Just how to give the child an integral world – that is the issue. It is also the spiritual issue of the modern religious personality. Among our most immediate tasks is to establish this new sense of the earth and of the human as a function of the earth.

We need to understand that the earth acts in all that acts upon the earth. The earth is acting in us whenever we act. In and through the earth spiritual energy is present. The spiritual energy emerges in the total complex of earth functions. Each form of life is integrated with every other life form. Even beyond the earth, by force of gravitation, every particle of the physical world attracts and is attracted to every other particle. This attraction holds the differentiated universe together and enables it to be a universe of individual realities. The universe is not a vast smudge of matter, some jelly-like substance extended indefinitely in space. Nor is the universe a collection of unrelated particles. The universe is, rather, a vast multiplicity of individual realities with both qualitative and quantitative differences all in spiritual-physical communion with each other. The individuals of similar form are bound together in their unity of form. The species are related to one another by derivation: the later, more complex life forms are derived from earlier, more simple life forms.

The first shaping of the universe was into those great galactic systems of fiery energy that constitute the starry heavens. In these celestial furnaces the elements are shaped. Eventually, after some ten billion years, the solar system and the earth and its living forms constituted a unique planet in the entire complex of the universe. Here on earth life, both plant and animal life, was born in the primordial seas some three billion years ago. Plants came out upon the land some six hundred million years ago, after the planet earth had shaped itself through a great series of transformations forming the continents, the mountains, the valleys, the rivers and streams. The atmosphere was long in developing. The animals came ashore a brief interval later. As these life forms established themselves over some hundreds of millions of years, the luxuriant foliage formed layer after layer of organic matter, which was then buried in the crust of the earth to become fossil formations with enormous amounts of stored energy. One hundred million years ago flowers appeared and the full beauty of earth began to manifest itself. Some sixty million years ago the birds were in the air. Mammals walked through the forest. Some of the mammals – the whales, porpoises, and dolphins – went back into the sea.

Finally, some two million years ago, the ascending forms of life culminated in the awakening human consciousness. Wandering food gatherers and hunters until some eight thousand years ago, we then settled into village life. This life led us through the neolithic period to the classical civilization which has flourished so brilliantly for the past five thousand years.

Then, some four hundred years ago, a new stage of scientific development took place which in the eighteenth and nineteenth centuries, brought about human technological dominance of the earth out of which we had emerged. This stage can be interpreted as the earth awakening to consciousness of itself in its human mode of being. The story of this awakening consciousness is the most dramatic aspect of the earth story.

The spiritual attitude that then caused or permitted humans to attack the earth with such savagery has never been adequately explained. That it was done by a Christian-derived society, and even with the belief that this was the truly human and Christian task, makes explanation especially harsh for our society.

Possibly it was the millennial drive toward a total transformation of the earth condition that led us, resentful that the perfect world was not yet achieved by divine means, to set about the violent subjugation of the earth by our own powers in the hope that in this way the higher life would be attained, our afflictions healed.

While this is the positive goal sought it must be added that the negative, even fearful, attitude toward the earth resulting from the general hardships of life led to the radical disturbance of the entire process. The increasing intensity shown in exploiting the earth was also the result of the ever-rising and unsatiated expectation of Western peoples. Even further, the natural tensions with the earth were increased by the Darwinian principle of natural selection, indicating that the primary attitude of each individual and each species is for its own survival at the expense of the others. Out of this strife, supposedly, the glorious achievements of the earth take place. Darwin had only minimal awareness of the cooperation and mutual dependence of each form of life on the other forms of life. This is amazing since he himself discovered the great web of life. Still, he had no real appreciation of the principle of intercommunion.

Much more needs to be said on the conditions that permitted such a mutually destructive situation to arise between ourselves and the earth, but we must pass on to give some indication of the new attitude that needs to be adopted toward the earth. This involves a new spiritual and even mystical communion with the earth, a true aesthetic of the earth, a sensitivity to earth needs, a valid economy of the earth. We need a way of designating the earth-human world in its continuity and identity rather than in its discontinuity and difference. In spirituality, especially, we need to recognize the numinous qualities of the earth. We might begin with some awareness of what it is to be human, or the role of consciousness on the earth, and of the place of the human species in the universe.

While the scholastic definition of the human as a rational animal gives us some idea of ourselves among the biological species, it gives us a rather inadequate sense of the role we play in the total earth process. The Chinese have a better definition of the human as the *hsin* of heaven and earth. This word *hsin* is written as a pictograph of the human heart. It should be translated by a single word or phrase with both a feeling and an understanding aspect. It could be thus translated by saying that the human is the 'understanding heart of heaven and earth'. Even more briefly, the phrase has been translated by Julia Ch'ing in the statement that the human is 'the heart of the universe.' It could, finally, be translated by saying that we are 'the consciousness of the world', or 'the psyche of the universe.' Here we have a remarkable feeling for the absolute dimensions of the human, the total integration of reality in the human, the total integration of the human within the reality of things.

We need a spirituality that emerges out of a reality deeper than ourselves, even deeper than life, a spirituality that is as deep as the earth process itself, a spirituality born out of the solar system and even out of the heavens beyond the solar system. There in the stars is where the primordial elements take shape in both their physical and psychic aspects. Out of these elements the solar system and the earth took shape, and out of the earth, ourselves.

There is a certain triviality in any spiritual discipline that does not experience itself as supported by the spiritual as well as the physical dynamics of the entire cosmic-earth process. A spirituality is a mode of being in which not only the divine and the human commune with each other, but we discover ourselves in the universe and the universe discovers itself in us. The Sioux Indian Crazy Horse called upon these depths of his being when he invoked the cosmic forces to support himself in battle. He painted the lightning upon his cheek, placed a rock behind his ear, an eagle feather in his hair, and the head of a hawk upon his head. Assumption of the cosmic insignia is also evident in the Sun Dance Ceremony. In this dance the symbols of the sun and moon and stars are cut out of rawhide and worn by the dancers. The world of living moving things is indicated by the form of the buffalo cut from rawhide, and by eagle feathers. The plant world is represented by the cottonwood tree set up in the center of the ceremonial circle. The supreme spirit itself is represented by the circular form of the dance area.

So the spiritual personality should feel constantly in communion with those numinous cosmic forces out of which we were born. Furthermore, the cosmic-earth order needs to be supplemented by the entire historical order of human development such as was depicted on the shield of Achilles by Homer and on the shield of Aeneas by Virgil. Virgil spends several long pages enumerating the past and future historical events wrought on the shield of Aeneas by Vulcan at the command of Venus, the heavenly mother of Aeneas. All these cosmic and historical forces are presently available to us in a new mode of appreciation. The historical and the cosmic can be seen as a single process. This vision of earth-human development provides the sustaining dynamic of the contemporary world.

3.2 Gaia and theology

Celia Deane-Drummond, 'God and Gaia: Myth or Reality?', *Theology*, 95, 766, 1992, pp. 278, 280–4

As life sciences have become more specialized into separate compartments, with biological research focused on an ultimate goal of interpretation according to the laws of mathematics, physics and chemistry, there has been a growing dis-ease with the meaningfulness of the exercise. The megasequencing of long stretches of DNA has become a kind of madness. Someone who was outside the biological world was bold enough to propagate an alternative approach to the living world. Jim Lovelock's space exploration convinced him that our planet is unique in its unusual atmospheric composition compared with other planets. The remarkable persistence of the earth in spite of its thermodynamic instability away from equilibrium led to his belief that the whole earth is a living being. The biosphere, which includes the atmosphere, acts as a single unit in such a way that environmental conditions are kept constant.

Lovelock is quite ready to admit that his ideas are not entirely new. As early as 1785 James Hutton proposed that the earth is a super-organism. While a holistic approach is characteristic of all physiological investigations, we are now dealing with physiology at the macro scale of the whole earth. Lovelock is convinced that the homeostatic processes which have kept environmental conditions constant over many millennia are maintained by active feedback processes from the biota. In order to test his hypothesis he proposed a model system where the earth's temperature could be kept constant by changing populations of white and black daisies. The white daisies reflect sunlight, while the black daisies absorb sunlight, leading to a corresponding cooling or warming of the atmosphere respectively. The system works automatically, and he believes that this is counter to his critics' charge that his theory is somehow 'teleological'.

. . .

Those who have taken Gaia beyond her scientific boundaries have ignored the fact that even if Gaia is 'living', she is not alive in the ordinary understanding of what being alive means. It is the popular understanding of Gaia as living being which is rooted in Greek mythology that gives Gaia its religious and theological undertones. Lovelock never intended his thesis to develop into a neo-Gaian mythology, though his own choice of language betrays a sympathy towards ancient/folk religious attitudes to nature.

Darwin's theory of evolution stressed the importance of individual populations, and the sheer diversity and complexity of speciation. Humankind became a part of nature, but in a way which still allowed us to perceive of ourselves as the climax to the whole process. Teilhard de Chardin could quite happily put forward a form of evolutionary theory which viewed the world as undergoing progressive development towards more complex and higher forms of life. Humanity's emergence was a great leap forward, and part of the same process leading to the climax of evolution in the coming of Christ. While Teilhard's notion of panpsychism overlaps with the idea of interconnectedness in Gaian thought, his insistence on the place of humankind as the crown of creation makes his overall perception of creation completely different.

Our increasing awareness of the destructiveness wrought on this earth by the human species has made many contemporary thinkers more cautious in adopting Teilhard's over-optimistic vision. The Gaia hypothesis seems to provide an alternative way of looking at the world, which relegates humankind to the position of 'a pathogenic parasite on the whole planetary organism', or more simply, 'a weed'. Lovelock is quite ready to admit that he is definitely not a favourite amongst the environmentalists. For if the earth is a self-regulatory organism, then the living Gaia will tend to ignore the pollutants we produce, until a new threshold is reached where there will be a drastic change in conditions such that humanity's existence is no longer assured. Humankind becomes eradicated, but Gaia, the real life of the planet, survives the sickness wrought by humanity.

It is this understanding of Gaia as living being against all the odds that seems to have encouraged Neo-Gaian ideas about adopting a lifestyle in tune with Gaia. She becomes the intelligent goddess, 'the earth spirit, she is life, the air, the water and the interaction between all their inhabitants'. Those who are uneasy about the superior status of Gaia are not reassured by Pedler's frank admission that he has 'sailed close to a restatement of pantheism'.

Once we begin to ask the question of whether Gaia will dispose of us we are saying that not only in the beginning God created heaven and earth with Gaia in mind, but that God, or rather Goddess, is Gaia. The Greek term for mother earth was Gaia or Ge. According to Hesiod, writing in about 700 BC, Gaia is the mother or grandmother of Zeus. His rule was dependent on her approval and consent. The priority of the female principle may partly explain why the Gaian theory finds a sympathetic audience amongst feminist writers wishing to re-image our understanding of God and creation according to feminine characteristics. It seems to me that this has been done largely in ignorance of the malevolent face of nature towards humanity that Lovelock's Gaia displays.

In historical terms our attitude to nature has shifted from one dominated by fear before the Enlightenment, to one where the desire for her conquest reduced nature to a machine. The Gaian movement raises fears characteristic of the more ancient mythology, though ironically Lovelock's inspiration for this concept came from use of highly sophisticated space technology. Darwin's theory of evolution encouraged a view of our natural world associated with progress towards higher forms, and seemed to remove any requirement for theistic creation. The storm of controversy amongst church leaders of his day reflects a greater readiness then to speak out on seeming threats to a traditional understanding of the theology of creation. Overall, however, Neo-Darwinists remained highly optimistic about our ability to modify the course of evolution, and so posed comparatively little threat to theological belief in the special dignity of humankind. Although many perceived Darwin's views as threatening, since they seemed to join our biological existence directly with the apes, while we could be viewed as part of nature the climax of evolution was still human existence. (The flowering of the molecular biology movement in the twentieth century betrays an almost romantic belief in the reductionist attitude to biology, which found its inspiration in Darwin's thesis.)

The future-orientated changing, evolving world envisaged by Darwin contrasts with the relatively stable picture of the world encouraged by the Gaian approach. For the latter imagines long periods of relatively little change 'punctuated' by short bursts of drastic change while the earth approaches a new steady state. There is no guarantee that human life will be part of the next 'stable state' of the earth, since according to Love-lock's theory the priority is the persistence of life, rather than human life. If we interpret Gaia according to Craik's dissipative theory, even life itself, in theory, could be under threat, since the next stable state depends on energy flow. Given the plasticity of microorganisms to adapt, it seems to me that we can assume life in some form will survive. Microorganisms assume an ascendency that would be impossible to conceive according to Darwin's theory of evolution.

The theological challenge of the Gaia hypothesis is that not only does it seem to remove the special place of humankind in creation, but also it is essentially pessimistic. Gaia does not have a 'moral' responsibility to preserve humankind. Pedler suggests that Gaia is a 'revolutionary' who is 'neither cruel, moral nor immoral. It cares nothing for the continuance of the human race and can design the death of man, woman or child as and when appropriate. It possesses ancient wisdom, is wholly integrated into its purpose and cannot be defeated, but only joined.' Hence the author remarks that Gaia is the most dangerous and determined opponent ever to face us. The harsh tone of Tennyson/Darwin's nature 'red in tooth and claw' seems relatively mild compared with the threat of the world organism turned against us.

Once more nature as malevolent seems to have surfaced in the con-sciousness of twentieth-century humankind. The New Age movement has welcomed the idea in Gaian theory that diversity is an aspect of unity, and believes that Gaia is a scientific basis for New Age ideology. How-ever, it has failed to recognize the inconsistency of Gaian thought with the New Age affirmation of human potential and individual self-improvement. The uncritical adoption of Gaian theory seems to depend on the mythical aspect of this theory, rather than its basis in science. In other words it seems to me more likely that the implicit attraction of Gaia for New Age thinkers is in its religious connotations associated with ancient Greek myth, rather than its value as science.

Once we believe that the earth has the power of a single living organ-ism to set the future for its component parts it becomes difficult to affirm belief in a loving Creator God who became incarnate in humanity. A trinitarian approach to the relationship between God and creation pre-vents Gaia from assuming too great an importance over and beyond a scientific hypothesis. The truth of the interconnectedness between all parts of creation that Gaia emphasizes in the wake of disillusionment with reductionist science, can be best expressed theologically since it is out-side the boundary of accessibility to scientific method. The service of theology to science becomes a reminder of the unity of all creation expressed in the doctrine of the immanence of God the Holy Spirit. Moltmann's alignment of God as Spirit with Gaia has ignored the mythological connotations of Gaia as well as its scientific limitations. While I agree with Moltmann's trinitarian approach to the relationship between God and creation, it seems to me that this challenges, rather than absorbs, Gaian thought.

The reversion to a view of the world which, logically, leads to a fearful and fateful attitude to human existence, denies the Christian hope in the future. Rather like the Darwinian theory which outgrew its place in the fashion for Evolutionism in the nineteenth century, Gaia needs to be 'tamed' if she is not to become 'too big for her boots'. Lovelock never intended Gaia to become a Goddess, though his enthusiasm for his idea has led to others to use Gaia as a scientific basis for a poetical and mystical view of the unity of the cosmos. It seems to me both that a green theology which takes account of the idea of Gaia needs to be realistic about its limits as science, and that Gaia should not be allowed a place as a form of theology. The spurious links between Gaia and mysticism are unhelpful both from the perspective of scientists, who then tend to reject Gaia altogether, and from the perspective of theologians, who revert to a form of pantheism under the guise of innovative science. While it is possible to identify with Gaia in its resistance to a dualistic approach to the material and spiritual world, a starting point in trinitarian theology offers a more promising way of overcoming such dualism, rather than through pseudo-science expressed in Neo-Lovelockian thought.

3.3 Attitudes to nature

Celia Deane-Drummond, 'Biology and Theology in Conversation: Reflections on Ecological Theology', *New Blackfriars*, 74, 865, 1993, pp. 469–73

Jürgen Moltmann insists that the way we think about God shapes patterns in our relationships with others and with nature. A traditional idea of God is that he is apathetic, that is he could not suffer, and that he is male, as Father. This view tended to invite the idea that God is an all-powerful tyrant who is remote from his creation. It is *not* the case that there are well developed theologies which describe God as Monarch in literalistic terms, rather the tendency is to stress the power of God, rather than his love. Moltmann is sensitive to this trend in the popular conception of God. An understanding of God which moves on from this is one which stresses the relationship in the Trinity as the most significant aspect of

God's being. Here God is God in relation, the Son and the Spirit are equal partners with the Father. A further, more controversial stage, is to envisage the Father in maternal terms as one who gives birth to the world. The world is in God, in pantheistic relation, while he still begets the Son. His motherly and fatherly roles are complemented by the Spirit, who is feminine and immanent in creation. The Son is in solidarity with the suffering and transfiguration of creation through the dialectic of cross and resurrection.

We find, according to Moltmann, a parallel development of anthropology alongside our view of God. If we think of God in categories of power it is easy to see ourselves as having the right to have dominion and rule over nature. Our perception of our task to master a threatening and wild nature was the impetus behind much of early science. If we move to a more cooperative understanding of the Trinity, our role becomes stewardship and responsibility. The third stage is one where the stress is on seeing ourselves as part of nature, we are in holistic relation to the rest of humanity and all of creation. In the final stage, which is linked with pantheism, we become indistinguishable from nature; here we arrive at biocentrism.

In environmental ethics our attitude to nature has a direct bearing on practical decisions. There are three broad ways of perceiving 'nature':

(a) In the first category we find nature treated as an object to be manipulated and used for human benefit. Here its value is instrumental and purely economic: nature is a resource for human benefit.

(b) Now nature is given some value in relation to ourselves, which is known as inherent value. This differs from the first category in that the aesthetic and other benefits of nature become valuable in a way which makes putting a price tag on different conservational programmes seem rather crude. Nature is to be loved and cared for by humans who act in responsible ways.

(c) The third stage, which is more 'biocentric', encourages a view of nature which gives it intrinsic value. This varies enormously in definition, here we mean value for its own sake quite apart from human interests.

(d) The final category, which encourages nature to have equal value to us, would lead logically to equal immorality being ascribed to killing or wounding any 'life', including the smallpox virus, which can only be biologically alive inside humans.

How does all this affect science and theology? The actual practice of science is logically possible in (a) to (c). Process theology was one of the early theological movements which was aware of the significance of the ecological crisis for theology. The justification of science now is that as evolved beings we are part of the process of the emergent Creator. Hence, pantheistic tendencies are heavily influenced by Darwinian ideas of evolutionary process. This tends to encourage a view which shows the common origin of all creatures, but in a way which still puts humankind at the culmination of this process. As such we still have a superior position: the world as a whole seems to yearn for greater enrichment of experience through humans and so it is less than fully biocentric.

The claim of process theology is, ironically, mixed in with an anti-anthropological stance. In other words, while the idea of the reverence for life, which J. Cobb accepts as the most fruitful way to think of creation, should lead to the absence of human domination through science, in fact it is often the way that scientists find is an acceptable concept of God, as it finds God expressed through subjective experience which is at its most advanced form in human experience. This gets rid of the troubling notion of God as other: the world is for human enrichment. Once the idea of God as other goes we start down the slippery slope of natural fatalism: resignation in the face of death and redundancy. More important, perhaps, is that the consequence of a failure to perceive God as other leads to the loss of the insight of the earth as gift. If creation is no longer a gift of God its value is subject to the vagaries of human opinion. Who is to decide which actions will lead to maximum enrichment? The strength of the traditional approach is that the real basis for the value of nature comes from its value in relationship to God. Moltmann reaches the same conclusion, even though in places he engages in dialogue with process thought.

The *Gaia* hypothesis of Lovelock is a strong challenge to the reductionist tendency in science. It envisages the whole geosphere acting like a giant organism. Many scientists find this hard to accept because it seems to draw on ancient cosmologies of the earth as a huge mystical body. While the more popular ideas of *Gaia* tend to portray this model in terms of the homeostatic regulation characteristic of the earth, it would be more accurate to view this process as rheostatic, that is bringing conditions back to preset norms. The value of Lovelock's idea lies in its encouragement to think and act globally. The difficulties are its basic anti-conservation and anti-anthropological stance. As long as *Gaia* survives, nothing else is considered important, humans become a cancer as far as the planet is concerned. While the science of Lovelock's ideas are refutable, *Gaia* is an important myth to be reckoned with theologically. But some other wisdom is needed once we face the practical ethical eco-logical decisions, for example choosing between some species rather than others, or deciding who is really responsible when the third world countries are forced to import polluting industries.

While Moltmann may be right in identifying religious commitments as those which have a profound effect on our attitudes to nature, his cat-egorization does not always show itself in history. For example, the love of animals was around in the early modern era long before our view of God began to change. A green theology would attempt to be a theology which is true to itself as theology: concerned with questions about God, but at the same time humble about the potential impact this might have on humanity or the globe at large. It is open to the world, including sci-ence, but would challenge the practice of science where it seems to weaken the dignity of other humans or creation. A 'biocentric' view is inadequate when it comes to hard practical choices of existence. How-ever, a holistic view, which values ecological systems, brings questions about ecological stability onto the agenda. The animal rights activists fail when it comes to a sense of value for communities.

A green theology would also welcome the example of science as that which is undertaken in collaboration with others. It is not just a matter of looking at problem texts in Genesis, but of opening up the dialogue between theology and other disciplines. Again, the advancement of science has often continued in this way; periods of specialisation need to be followed by a period of cooperation. Habermas has given us a philosophical basis for this approach, while Moltmann has given us a theological foundation through his understanding of the social Trinity. If the concept of stewardship has failed, since it still allows the idea of the instrumental value of nature to be retained, a simple resacralisation of nature will fail because it denies human responsibility. A combination of respect for nature with holiness is the ideal portrayed by the early Church, especially the Celtic saints. A sense of the sacred on its own leads to inaction and a failure to confront the issues of human injustice which are bound up with questions about the environment.

Carol J. Adams, 'Introduction', in Carol J. Adams (ed.), *Ecofeminism and the Sacred*, New York, Continuum, 1993, pp. 1–3

For many years now, women around the world have worked to transform a social order that sanctions human oppression and environmental abuse. We see the interrelationship of social domination and the domination of the rest of nature, such as deforestation that displaces indigenous peoples; hazardous waste sites located near poor and Black neighbourhoods; industrialized factory farms that eliminate the small family farmer; and international policies of free trade that hurt poor people and the earth. Women are the major caretakers of victims of pollution, and along with the poor they are the primary victims of industrial pollution. The overwhelming majority of the millions of people denied the basic rights of clean air, water, food, shelter, health, and well-being are women. Aimed at both preventing and solving environmental problems, our responses have included designing solar cookers and greenhouses, transforming farming methods that damaged the environment, challenging loggers, analyzing economic policies that fail to measure environmental protection (or housework) as 'productive,' holding vigils outside of slaughterhouses, investigating chemical dumping, protesting war and the military-industrial complex.

The term *ecofeminism* defines these global activisms and analyses.

Ecofeminism*s* might be more accurate in conveying the diversity of these responses to environmental exploitation.

Ecofeminism identifies the twin dominations of women and the rest of nature. To the issues of sexism, racism, classism, and heterosexism that concern feminists, ecofeminists add naturism – the oppression of the rest of nature. Ecofeminism argues that the connections between the oppression of women and the rest of nature must be recognized to understand adequately both oppressions.

Some of the earliest feminist theologies in this wave of feminism examined attitudes toward the rest of nature, and some of the earliest ecofeminist texts critiqued religion. They demonstrated how metaphors of patriarchy simultaneously feminize nature and naturalize women. When patriarchal spirituality associates women, body, and nature, and then emphasizes transcending the body and transcending the rest of nature, it makes oppression sacred. Thus, since the publication in the 1970s of Rosemary Radford Ruether's *New Woman/New Earth* and Elizabeth Dodson Gray's *Green Paradise Lost*, analysis of theological constructs that contribute to women's and the rest of nature's oppression has been a vital part of ecofeminist writings.

In describing ecofeminism's focus, Karen J. Warren has identified a 'logic of domination', according to which, 'superiority justifies subordination':

> Ecofeminists insist that the sort of logic of domination used to justify the domination of humans by gender, racial, or ethnic, or class status is also used to justify the domination of nature. Because eliminating

a logic of domination is part of a feminist critique – whether a critique of patriarchy, white supremacist culture, or imperialism – ecofeminists insist that *naturism* is properly viewed as an integral part of any feminist solidarity movement to end sexist oppression and the logic of domination which conceptually grounds it. (In *Environmental Ethics*, 12, 3, 1990, p. 132)

This logic of domination is often expressed in dualisms.

Dualisms reduce diversity to two categories: A or Not A. They convey the impression that everything can then be appropriately categorized: *either* it is A *or* Not A. These dualisms represent dichotomy rather than continuity, enacting exclusion rather than inclusion. Ecofeminists analyze many restrictive dualisms that uphold a logic of domination: independence/interdependence; heaven/earth; male/female; culture/nature; mind/body; white/'non-white'; humans/animals; humans/nature.

Ecofeminism has traced the dualisms that characterize Eurocentric patriarchal culture to (1) classical thought and Jewish and Christian religious traditions (see the work of Ruether and Gray), (2) the modern European mechanistic science and Enlightenment philosophy emphasizing autonomy and objective knowing (see the work of Merchant and Easlea), or (3) the desacralization of the Earth in favour of a sky-god (Spretnak, Starhawk).

False dualisms result in several patriarchal theological tenets: transcendence and domination of the natural world, fear of the body, projection of evil upon women, world-destroying spiritual views. Moreover, the second part of the dualism is not only subordinate but *in service* to the first. Women serve men; nature serves culture; animals serve humans; people of color serve white people. Ecofeminists seek a transformed consciousness that eliminates the dualisms that undergird dominance. We note, for instance, that the same dominant mind-set that separates humans from the rest of nature divides politics from spirituality, as though humans are not a part of nature and politics is not integrally related to spirituality. The matter/spirit, politics/spirituality dualisms are a product of Western theology and philosophy. The voices of women of color and women from other philosophical traditions offer alternative metaphysical viewpoints in which the matter/spirit dualism evaporates.

Because of the ecofeminist analysis that attributes the degradation of nature to the dominant Euro-American worldview, indigenous and non-technological cultures have been sources for the creation of syncretistic ecofeminist spiritualities. Many ecofeminists look to earth-based spiritualities as alternatives to dominant theologies. *How* to incorporate diverse cultural and religious traditions within ecofeminism is an important ethical/political question to raise about these syncretistic efforts. The more diverse the sources for envisioning ecofeminist spiritualities, the more opportunities exist for either succumbing to racism or exposing racism in this syncretism.

3.4 Cosmic relationships

Richard A. Young, *Healing the Earth: A Theocentric Perspective on Environmental Problems and their Solutions*, Nashville, Tennessee, Broadman & Holman, 1994, pp. 60–4

A popular way among New Age enthusiasts to perceive the interrelatedness of the natural order is the Gaia hypothesis. The Gaia hypothesis as formulated by the British scientist James Lovelock depicts the earth as behaving like one gigantic organism. . . . He rejected the idea common among some advocates of the hypothesis that there is a global mind governing the planet's self-regulating processes, saying rather that the process is accomplished through a complex set of cause-effect feedback relations. Thus the earth is not a living organism, it only behaves like one. Although scientists debate the validity of some points of the hypothesis, the general outline seems to correspond with the basic operation of ecosystems.

New Age writers have taken the Gaia hypothesis much further than the purely scientific level that Lovelock proposed and given it mystical connotations. The earth not only behaves like a living organism, it is a living organism. Some add that Gaia is a conscious organism, with which people can communicate. One example would be the communications of the Findhord community with the Devas. The idea that the earth is a living, conscious organism is found among many native peoples, who communicate with the rivers and mountains. In *Minding the Earth*, Joseph Meeker refrains from using the term *Gaia* because it implies that the universe is personal, as the goddess' name suggests. Nevertheless Meeker contends that we can 'enter into conversation with it.'

A third level of Gaia interpretation, a natural step from the second level, is to attribute divinity to the earth. Shamanic cultures affirm that the earth is a sacred being, the body of deity, and something to be worshiped. Most think of it as a female deity, a mother that has given birth to all life. Biblical prophets vehemently denounced such pagan nature worship. The idea of a divine cosmos cannot be reconciled with the Judeo-Christian God who created the cosmos and exists apart from it.

But in what sense, if at all, can the earth be considered a living organism? Just because it supports individual life forms or even a global ecosystem does not warrant its being termed a living organism any more than the homes in which we live can be called living beings because they are 'alive' with creatures within. If the earth were a living being, it must be of a higher, more complex order than humans, and yet the simple observation remains that the earth is not a sentient being; it does not have intelligence, feelings, or volition. Furthermore, if the earth were a living organism, it should be able to reproduce itself as other living organisms do. The observation that the earth's processes respond in a cause-effect manner to stimuli does not imply that it is a self-conscious organism any more than billiard balls responding when they are struck suggest that they are alive.

The most we can say is that the earth behaves like a living organism, that it is alive in the sense of being 'alive' with living creatures, or that it constitutes an environment supportive of life. Daniel Botkin wrote:

> We are accustomed to thinking of life as a characteristic of individual organisms. Individuals are alive, but an individual cannot sustain life. Life is sustained only by a group of organisms of many species – not simply a horde or mob, but a certain kind of system composed of many individuals of different species – and their environment, making together a network of living and nonliving parts that can maintain the flow of energy and the cycling of chemical elements that, in turn, support life. (*Discordant Harmonies*, New York, Oxford University Press, 1990, p. 7)

In this sense we could expand the concept of life to the entire earth, without calling the earth a living organism. The Gaia hypothesis is actually counterproductive to environmentalism, for if Gaia were truly self-healing, then there would be no need for human intervention to try to correct the imbalances.

The Scriptures contain a wealth of resources to substantiate the idea that all reality is interrelated and forms one integrated ecosystem. The biblical view that living organisms are individual, interrelated, and dependent on proper relations within an ecosystem is perfectly compatible with the modern scientific understanding of ecology and the four laws of ecology expressed by Barry Commoner. The biblical view, moreover, expands the concept of interrelatedness to include the spiritual dimension. Just as trees cannot exist apart from their ecosystem, nor humanity apart from nature, neither can either one exist apart from God.

God created the entire natural order as a complex interrelated ecosystem that cannot exist in isolation from His sustaining influence.

The unity and interrelatedness of all creation can best be explained in terms of a single Creator. If there were two or more gods, or no God at all, then there would be the possibility of divergent ecological structures in different parts of the earth. Yet there is only one structure or one set of principles governing ecological processes. The observation that the universe is a single interlocking network of life forms in which one part cannot exist independently of the rest argues for the existence of a single Creator. If everything has been set in motion by a single Creator, a Creator who cannot act contrary to His nature as a harmonious triune God, then everything at its conception must reflect the Creator and constitute a single harmonious cosmic community with singleness of design and structure. When everything is perceived as cocreatures and coinhabitants of a cosmic community, we can echo the canticle of Saint Francis and speak of Brother Sun and Sister Moon. It is only within this cosmic community, which has God as its head, that we will find full realization of ourselves as social beings.

A term often employed to designate the unity and harmony of the created realm within Christian circles is 'integrity of creation.' The term 'signifies an attempt to rediscover a sense of the wholeness of the creation in relation to God and the need for ethical imperatives towards renewal and at-oneness'. These ethical imperatives are based on the functional structure of the universe, which in turn is based on the very character of the Creator. In this sense we can speak of the creation as an extension of the Creator. Everything works in harmony when it works by the moral and ecological laws established by God. When these laws are broken, the relations between parts are severed, and the whole ceases to function as God intended. One's quest must be to find those laws that govern relationships. Finding these laws will produce wholeness and health not only to the environment but to the individual and society as well. The healing web of relationships, however, must extend beyond the physical to the spiritual and include a proper relationship with God.

The Bible is preeminently a book about relationships. This is evident from the use of relational terms and themes throughout Scripture, terms such as *covenant, love, hate, sin, grace, faith, hope, redemption, salvation*, and *reconciliation*. Sittler noted that 'each of these is a term that points to the establishment of a relationship, or the breaking of a relationship, or the perversion of a relationship; and each one points to the promise of blessedness as the reestablishment of a relationship.' *Sin* is the primary negative relational term in Scripture. Other negative relational terms such as *anger, hatred, greed,* and *fornication* are subsumed under *sin,* for all tend to sever relations. These relational terms apply to nature as well as humanity.

The biblical concept of salvation suggests wholeness and healing. It refers to the restoring of peace and harmony through the person and work of Christ. It is a healing of broken relations, first between God and humanity, then between humans, and finally between humanity and nature. We are called on to participate in the healing of our broken and fragmented world (2 Cor. 5:18–20) and to work out our salvation in all aspects of life (Phil. 2:12). The biblical notion of salvation is an ecological concept that pertains to the restoration of all relationships that were severed at the fall. That the whole cosmos is included in this salvation is evident from Romans 8:21 where creation itself is to be 'liberated from its bondage to decay and brought into the glorious freedom of the children of God.'

The relationships between God, humanity, and nature could be conceived as a triangle. When one side of the ecological triangle is broken, it shatters the other sides as well, for the triangle will function properly only if it remains whole. For example, when we rebel against God, it severs our relation with nature, since we will ignore God's injunction to care for the earth, and nature's relation with God, since God will judge the disobedient through nature, as witnessed by the deluge. Although God is able to heal all these relations, He will do so only in response to our choice. The relations were broken by humanity and cannot be fully restored in the present era without our choosing to return to God, the Creator and Sustainer of all life.

Within the larger spectrum of biblical ecology, we cannot say that everything that exists is interdependent, for this would include God. The Scriptures make a necessary distinction between the Creator and the creation, setting God apart as infinite, self-sustaining, and not dependent on anything else (see Heb. 9:11). The entire created realm is finite, contingent, and thus dependent for its continued existence on something other than itself. The chain of dependencies reaches up to the Apex, or to the self-sustaining Fountainhead of all life, but does not include Him in the network of interdependencies. If God were included in a cosmic web of interdependencies, then He would be the finite god of process theology and not the infinite God of the Scriptures. The ecological triangle is therefore a triangle of relationships, not a triangle of interdependencies.

3.5 Against pantheism and naturism

Stephen R. L. Clark, *How to Think about the Earth: Philosophical and Theological Models for Ecology*, London, Mowbray, 1993, p. 29

Mainstream biologists are usually dismissive of 'Gaia': 'a metaphor, not a mechanism', according to Steven J. Gould, or (yet more contemptuously) a surrender to the 'BBC Documentary Syndrome', whereby all is for the best in the best of all possible worlds (as Richard Dawkins asserts). Quite why the hypothesis has been dismissed so eagerly is not wholly clear. 'A metaphor': but so also is 'natural selection', and 'mechanism'. 'An excuse for thinking all is for the best': but Lovelock expressly and repeatedly emphasizes that the feed-back mechanisms he postulates are not directed at *our* survival, nor consciously directed at all, and that the teleological account he gives (as that the output of dimethyl sulphide by marine algae plays a major role in the transport of sulphur from the sea to the land, and so in the maintenance of land-life) rests upon a straightforwardly biochemical study of the mechanisms involved. The question is, what regulates that production, and would we have noticed it at all without having sought to find out how land-life can have got the sulphur that it needs? Plants do not photosynthesize 'to produce oxygen for us' (in Dawkins' mocking summary), but the whole system is now as dependent on their doing so as ever our personal survival is on the regulated production of our necessary hormones.

Stephen R. L. Clark, 'Is Nature God's Will?', in Andrew Linzey and Dorothy Yamamoto (eds), *Animals on the Agenda: Questions about Animals for Theology and Ethics*, London, SCM, 1998, pp. 125–8

Both the theory and mainstream reaction to it [*the 'Gaia hypothesis'*] suggest to some, and especially to those already disenchanted with modern technocratic civilization, that there are other forms of knowledge than the merely rational or objective. We know the world best when we *feel* with it, when we recognize it from within, as part and parcel of a multi-millionfold experiment in being. Its most enthusiastic supporters see Gaia as a counter-example to the neo-Darwinian notion that providence plays no part in things, and also to the merely anthropocentric fantasy that it is our advantage that such a providence provides. In that sense the 'Television Documentary Syndrome' (that all is for the best in this best of all possible worlds) does have a part to play in the acceptance of the hypothesis: not that the world is the best there is for us, but that we should reorganize our moral perceptions so as to think that what is good for Gaia is the only or pre-eminent good. So Gaia either is itself the thing most worth admiring or it is the best available image of cooperative, synergistic life, the Mother.

But before we accept the Living Earth and Nature as our guide, in the guise of Gaia or the Mother Goddess, we should consider the historical associations of that creed. The charge against traditional religion, that it has inhumane or destructive associations, can, unfortunately, be turned round: this century (as Ikeda hinted) saw the rise and fall of a movement that actually shared a great many of the doctrines and evaluations typical of Toynbee's pantheistic environmentalism, namely Nazism [*Arnold Toynbee, 1889–1975, British writer and historian*]. Consider the following compendious account of modern 'naturism' (a term now associated with high-principled nudism – whose roots are not so far from the ideology I aim to describe). [*A different use of 'naturism' from pp. 76–7 above.*] The 'natural' (which is to say the living) world is perfect in its beauty, not to be disparaged or renounced in the name of any other or transcendental world. There is a 'balance of nature' which can be momentarily upset but which will (with more or less inevitability) swing back. 'Human beings', as a class, are no more than one temporary – and heterogeneous – species amongst the many strands that make up the biosphere. The 'techno-logical fix' is to be distrusted partly because it favours the delusion that 'no man need pay for his sins', and partly because technology in the modern manner is founded on the assumption that the world can be managed 'mechanically' rather than 'organically' and with due attention to the 'spirit within'. Some human beings have been misled – usually by Jews and Christians, but sometimes by Hellenists – into thinking that they have special rights or dignities, but our best image of the 'Divine' is not human, but either the Earth herself, Gaia, or the multitudinous spirits of wood and river, spring-time and leaf-fall, sex, death and affection. For similar reasons merely legal or official authority, the kind of authority that depends on office or abstract law, is of less significance than charismatic or national authority. The 'real' person, and the 'real' world, are ones stripped of all 'merely cultural or historical' significance, so that naked-ness is indeed of more than 'hygienic' or 'aesthetic' importance.

Let me emphasize the most embarrassing association. The humankind that is most deadly to the world – so pantheistic environmentalists will often say – is individualistic, capitalistic, deracinated and influenced by the dreams of human grandeur purveyed – supposedly – in the Jewish scriptures. As Toynbee said: we must discard Judaic monotheism, and prefer the sort of rooted love of earth and its spirits that pantheism or paganism stands for. Instead of treating land as real estate to be transformed to abstract capital we must live within our limits, acknowledging the ties of kinship and the love of earthly beauty. The real cause of plague lies in the Jewish heritage of civilized humanity: we must root out its causes – *which is just what Hitler said*. It would not take much for the notions that humankind is, as presently constituted, a plague, and that it is all – somehow – the fault of the Jews (deracinated intellectuals and capitalistic usurers), to merge in anti-semitism of Hitler's kind. The Nazis did not treat Jews (and Gypsies) as animals (Hitler disapproved – though, as usual, incoherently – of hunting, flesh-eating and vivisection), but – exactly – as bacterial infections. Popular environmentalism of the kind purveyed in television documentaries continues, despite a hundred refutations, to blame 'Christianity' or 'the Jewish scriptures' for our arrogance in neglecting the rightful claims of nature.

The fact that there have been pantheists, or anti-theists, who have been guilty of atrocious crimes is not, of course, enough to refute those versions of environmentalism, or neo-paganism. So after all have Christians, Marxists, Pagans and 'postmodernists'. 'Just because something happens to have been emphasized by people as despicable as the Nazis does not make it wrong.' But we clearly need to ask whether pantheism offers a viable alternative to more humanistic ideologies: how naturist can good Christian theists be?

A good many such theists are very sympathetic to naturism. Non-Christian naturists regularly blame 'the Judaeo-Christian patriarchalist tradition' for Western assaults on nature. Christian naturists prefer to blame 'the Greeks'. All insist that true doctrine rejects any split between Spirit and Nature, the Eternal and the Here-and-Now. Many suggest that we are wrong to distinguish 'substances' and 'processes'. Jewish or Christian stories and doctrines that seem to imply otherwise must be interpreted 'metaphorically' if they are to be acceptable: notions like 'Original Sin', 'Fallen World', 'the World to Come' are suspect (unless they refer to capitalist corruptions of human nature, and the classless future). Christian naturists may retain some notion that there is an Outside, and that Humanity is a crucial link between this World and God ('the world's High Priest'), but worship of that Outside is – in the modern style – generally to be equated with 'love of the neighbour', action in the world, and not any 'flight of the Alone to the Alone'. All too often even that 'neighbour-love' amounts only to an insistence on 'togetherness' and 'socializing the economy'.

If Gaia, the Whole Earth, is a living organism, 'the Earth Mother', are we to be equated with the tissues, or organs, necessary to its survival or integrity? Or must we be considered something like a bacterial infection, an alien intrusion or cancerous growth? According to some versions, humankind is the mind and voice of Gaia, the 'growing point of evolution', the grand experiment to try out conscious thought as a mechanism for Gaia's future life. Pierre Teilhard de Chardin convinced some that evolutionary history was headed toward the increased 'complexity' of intellectual and social life, that it would culminate in the 'noosphere' – and lesser forms of humankind would be only failed experiments, perhaps to be disposed of. Gaia, wild nature, was to be fulfilled by being fully understood and tamed in human civilization. Modern pantheistic environmentalists would probably think de Chardin's vision unduly anthropocentric – as mainstream biologists always thought it unduly optimistic in imagining that 'evolution' had a fixed direction. But some would still suggest that human beings are justified by the contribution they can make to Gaia – and judged by their failure to contribute.

Topics for discussion

1 What is the relationship between a Christian understanding of creation and the domination of the natural world? Do you think that a spirituality that emphasizes the integrated nature of the created world would better serve a responsible ecological theology? Are the domination of nature and the patriarchal domination of women caused by the same logic of oppression?

2 Is it 'a fundamental theological truth for a Christian' that the world is a living thing? Are there any elements of the Gaia hypothesis that might be compatible with, and helpful for, a Christian ecological theology? Which elements of the Gaia hypothesis are incompatible with the doctrine of creation?

3 Is the Gaia hypothesis scientific or theological in nature? What are the implications of the Gaia hypothesis for a doctrine of providence? Does the Gaia hypothesis address the needs of the present ecological crisis more fully than the Christian theology?

4 Does a trinitarian approach to the doctrine of creation challenge or confirm the insights of the Gaia hypothesis? Is it important that Christian theology adopts an ethically responsible stance with regard to the created world? Does Jürgen Moltmann's trinitarian theology provide the resources for a responsible ecological theology?

5 Does the Bible provide the relevant material on which to base an ecological theology or, in the age of science, are biblical views to be regarded as primitive and redundant? In what ways is the Gaia hypothesis compatible or incompatible with *biblical* views of the created world?

6 Is the Gaia hypothesis a timely reminder that 'rational' explanations of the status of the rational world are not enough? What is the status of human beings in the Gaia hypothesis? What is the status of human beings in the Christian doctrine of creation?

4 Christian creation?

4.1 Creation in the New Testament

John 1:1–14

1 [1]In the beginning was the Word, and the Word was with God, and the Word was God. [2]He was in the beginning with God. [3]All things came into being through him, and without him not one thing came into being. What has come into being [4]in him was life, and the life was the light of all people. [5]The light shines in the darkness, and the darkness did not overcome it.

[6]There was a man sent from God, whose name was John. [7]He came as a witness to testify to the light, so that all might believe through him. [8]He himself was not the light, but he came to testify to the light. [9]The true light, which enlightens everyone, was coming into the world.

[10]He was in the world, and the world came into being through him; yet the world did not know him. [11]He came to what was his own, and his own people did not accept him. [12]But to all who received him, who believed in his name, he gave power to become children of God, [13]who were born, not of blood or of the will of the flesh or of the will of man, but of God.

[14]And the Word became flesh and lived among us, and we have seen his glory, the glory as of a father's only son, full of grace and truth.

Romans 8:18–24

[18]I consider that the sufferings of this present time are not worth comparing with the glory about to be revealed to us. [19]For the creation waits with eager longing for the revealing of the children of God; [20]for the creation was subjected to futility, not of its own will but by the will of the one who subjected it, in hope [21]that the creation itself will be set free from its bondage to decay and will obtain the freedom of the glory of the children

of God. [22]We know that the whole creation has been groaning in labour pains until now; [23]and not only the creation, but we ourselves, who have the first fruits of the Spirit, groan inwardly while we wait for adoption, the redemption of our bodies. [24]For in hope we were saved. Now hope that is seen is not hope. For who hopes for what is seen?

4.2 Creation in Barth

Karl Barth, *Church Dogmatics*, I, 1, ET Edinburgh, T & T Clark, 1975, pp. 390–1

God is unknown as our Father, as the Creator, to the degree that He is not made known by Jesus. . . .

If this exclusiveness is accepted and taken seriously, if that abstraction between form and content is thus seen to be forbidden, this rules out the possibility of regarding the first article of the Christian faith as an article of natural theology. Jesus' message about God the Father must not be taken to mean that Jesus expressed the well-known truth that the world must have and really has a Creator and was venturing to give this Creator the familiar human name of father. It must not be taken to mean that Jesus had in mind what all serious philosophy has called the first cause or supreme good, the *esse a se* or *ens perfectissimum*, the universum, the ground and abyss of meaning, the unconditioned, the limit, the critical negation or origin, and that He consecrated it and gave it a Christian interpretation and baptised it by means of the name 'father,' which was not entirely unknown in the vocabulary of religion. In this regard we can only say that this entity, the supposed philosophical equivalent of the Creator God, has nothing whatever to do with Jesus' message about God the Father whether or not the term 'father' be attached to it. Nor would it have anything to do with it even if the principle: Die and become! were related and perhaps identified with the transcendent origin and goal of the dialectic of losing life and gaining it. An idea projected with the claim that it is an idea of God is from the standpoint of the exclusiveness of the biblical testimonies an idol, not because it is an idea but because of its claim. Even the genuinely pure and for that very reason treacherously pure idea of God in a Plato cannot be excluded. If the exclusiveness is valid, Jesus did not proclaim the familiar Creator God and interpret Him by the unfamiliar name of Father. He revealed the unknown Father, His Father, and in so doing, and only in so doing, He told us for the first time that the Creator is, what He is and that He is as such our Father.

Karl Barth, *Church Dogmatics*, III, 1, ET Edinburgh, T & T Clark, 1958, pp. 3–4, 95–6, 231–2

... [T]he doctrine of the creation no less than the whole remaining content of Christian confession is an article of faith, i.e., the rendering of a knowledge which no man has procured for himself or ever will; which is neither native to him nor accessible by way of observation and logical thinking; for which he has no organ and no ability; which he can in fact achieve only in faith; but which is actually consummated in faith, i.e., in the reception of and response to the divine witness, so that he is made to be strong in his weakness, to see in his blindness and to hear in his deafness by the One who, according to the Easter story, goes through closed doors. It is a faith and doctrine of this kind which is expressed when in and with the whole of Christendom we confess that God is the Creator of Heaven and earth.

. . .

Creation is the freely willed and executed positing of a reality distinct from God. The question thus arises: What was and is the will of God in doing this? We may reply that he does not will to be alone in His glory; that He desires something else beside Him. But this answer cannot mean that God either willed or did it for no purpose, or that He did so to satisfy a need. Nor does it mean that He did not will to be and remain alone because He could not do so. And the idea of something beside Him which would be what it is independently of Him is quite inconsistent with His freedom. In constituting this reality He cannot have set a limit to His glory, will and power. As the divine Creator He cannot have created a remote and alien sphere abandoned to itself or to its own teleology. If, then, this positing is not an accident, if it corresponds to no divine necessity and does not in any sense signify a limitation of His own glory, there remains only the recollection that God is the One who is free in His love. In this case we can understand the positing of this reality – which otherwise is incomprehensible – only as the work of His love. He wills and posits the creature neither out of caprice nor necessity, but because He has loved it from eternity, because He wills to demonstrate His love for it, and because He wills, not to limit His glory by its existence and being, but to reveal and manifest it in His own co-existence with it. As the Creator He wills really to exist for His creature. That is why He gives it its own existence and being. That is also why there cannot follow from the creature's own existence and being an immanent determination of its goal or purpose, or a claim to any right, meaning or dignity of its existence and nature accruing to it except as a gift. That is why even the very existence and nature of the creature are the work of the grace of God. It would be a strange love that was satisfied with the mere existence and nature of the other, then withdrawing, leaving it to its own devices. Love wills to love. Love wills something with and for that which it loves. Because God loves the creature, its creation and continuance and preservation point beyond themselves to an exercise and fulfilment of His love which do not take place merely with the fact that the creature is posited as such and receives its existence and being alongside and outside the being and existence of God, but to which creation in all its glory looks and moves, and of which creation is the presupposition.

. . .

Creation is one long preparation, and therefore the being and existence of the creature one long readiness, for what God will intend and do with it in the history of the covenant. Its nature is simply its equipment for grace. Its creatureliness is pure promise, expectation and prophecy of that which in His grace, in the execution of the will of His eternal love, and finally and supremely in the consummation of the giving of His Son, God plans for man and will not delay to accomplish for his benefit. In this way creation is the road to the covenant, its external power and external basis, because for its fulfilment the latter depends wholly on the fact that the creature is in no position to act alone as the partner of God, that it is thrown back wholly and utterly on the care and intercession of God Himself, but that it does actually enjoy this divine care and intercession. What we now see is that the covenant is the internal basis of creation. . . . This consists in the fact that the wisdom and omnipotence of God the Creator was not just any wisdom and omnipotence but that of His free love . . . The fact that the covenant is the goal of creation is not something which is added later to the reality of the creature . . . It already characterises creation itself and as such, and therefore the being and existence of the creature. The covenant whose history had still to commence was the covenant which, as the goal appointed for creation and the creature, made creation necessary and possible, and determined and limited the creature. If creation was the external basis of the covenant, the latter was the internal basis of the former. If creation was the formal presupposition of the covenant, the latter was the material presupposition of the former. If creation takes precedence historically, the covenant does so in substance.

Karl Barth, *Church Dogmatics*, IV, 1, ET Edinburgh, T & T Clark, 1956, pp. 9–10

The ordaining of salvation for man and of man for salvation is the original and basic will of God, the ground and purpose of His will as Creator. It is not that He first wills and works the being of the world and man, and then ordains it to salvation. But God creates, preserves and over-rules man for this prior end and with this prior purpose, that there may be a being distinct from Himself ordained for salvation, for perfect being, for participation in His own being, because as the One who loves in freedom He has determined to exercise redemptive grace – and that there may be an object of this His redemptive grace, a partner to receive it. . . . The 'God with us' has nothing to do with chance. As a redemptive happening it means the revelation and confirmation of the most primitive relationship between God and man, that which was freely determined in eternity by God Himself before there was any created being. In the very fact that man is, and that he is man, he is as such chosen by God for salvation . . .

4.3 Redemptive, directive creation

Gregory Baum, *Man Becoming: God in Secular Experience*, New York, Seabury, 1979, pp. 200–3

Out of this experience of God as creator and ruler of the people, Israel came to raise the question of God's relationship to the cosmos. Israel's understanding of creation was an extension of its own redemptive experience. From the beginning the Israelites had listened to the creation stories told among the tribes and peoples that surrounded them, but they found it difficult to reconcile these stories with their view of God the redeemer. These stories presented the divinity engaged in conflict with other powers, with monsters inhabiting the ocean or with other chaotic forces, a conflict which gave rise to the creation of the world. The Old Testament bears occasional traces of these ancient stories. But with greater consistency the prophets of Israel tried to relate the creation of the cosmos to their saviour God: they presented creation as God's marvelous work preceding, announcing, and validating his marvelous work of the covenant. 'Awake, awake, put on your strength, O arm of the Lord! Awake as in the days of old, as in generations long gone. Was it not thou that didst hew Raheb (the sea monster) in pieces, that didst pierce the dragon? Was it not thou that didst dry up the sea, the waters of the mighty deep, that didst make the depth of the sea a way for the redeemed to pass over?' (Is. 51, 9–10). This passage refers to an ancient creation story, yet offers a soteriological interpretation of it. The God who showed his power in the covenant and the establishment of the people was operative in the creation of the world and is still operative in the present history of Israel.

In dialogue with the Babylonian creation stories, Israel eventually developed its own accounts of God's creation of the cosmos. These accounts are recorded on the opening pages of the Bible. But even these accounts are an extension into the past of Israel's redemptive understanding of its own genesis; they convey a redemptive message. They lead almost directly into the story of Abraham, the ancestor of Israel, and they present the creation of the cosmos according to the seven-day week of Israel's liturgical feasts. 'Presumptuous as it may sound, creation is part of the aetiology of Israel' (von Rad). The creation stories recorded in the book of Genesis represent the effort of the Hebrew prophets to relate their faith in the redeemer God of Israel to the origin of the whole world and to proclaim that Jahweh, the true God, who created and still creates the people of Israel, also created the cosmos. The creation of the world at the beginning of time is simply the antecedent to the covenant of grace.

Among the theologians of the twentieth century, it was above all Karl Barth who brought this result of biblical scholarship to the awareness of the Christian Church. In his vast theological system, based on the biblical research of his day, he presented the creation of the world as the preparation for, and presupposition of, the bestowal of grace. The goal of creation is the redemptive covenant. Only in Jesus Christ, therefore, is the meaning of creation fully revealed to us. Only in him is the nature of man fully disclosed. This theological approach, a turn-about in the history of Christian thought, enabled Karl Barth to overcome the unhappy tradition of distinguishing between creation and redemption as between two distinct modes or steps of divine activity.

The two-step distinction between creation and redemption prevented Christian theologians from explaining how the redemption brought by Christ was related to man's historical existence. If theologians began with the doctrine of creation and looked upon the world as the work of God, they tended to regard redemption as an extrinsic addition to natural life or an elevation above it. Catholics often followed this line. If theologians, on the other hand, began with the doctrine of redemption, they found it extremely difficult to acknowledge the goodness of creation and often tended to look upon the natural order as hostile to the divine. Protestants often followed this road. Karl Barth overcame this dilemma by adopting from the scriptures, understood in the light of modern historical scholarship, the soteriological understanding [of] creation. God is first of all redeemer: even his creation initiates redemption.

While, as we have said, it has become customary in traditional theology to make a clear distinction between creation and redemption, the scriptures do not always do this. Second Isaiah in particular unites the redemptive and creative action of God so intimately that creation often becomes a synonym for redemption. Creation is proclaimed as witness and pledge of God's present salvation. The prophet refers to the creation of the world as the sign that God is the redeemer of Israel in both past and present. 'Thus says the Lord, the God who created the heavens, and stretched them out, who made the earth and its products, who gives breath to the people upon it, and the spirit to those who walk in it: I the Lord have called you in righteousness and have grasped you by the hand' (Is. 42, 5–6). 'Thus says the Lord your redeemer, who formed you from the womb: I, the Lord, the maker of all, who stretched out the heavens above . . .' (Is. 44, 24). . . . Redemption and creation become synonymous. 'Thus says the Lord, who created you, O Jacob, and formed you, O Israel: Fear not, for I have redeemed you; I have called you by your name: you are mine' (Is. 43, 1).

Paul Tillich, *Systematic Theology*, I, London, Nisbet, 1953, pp. 292–3

The question whether the relation between God and the world should be expressed in terms of immanence or transcendence is usually answered by an 'as well as.' Such an answer, although it is correct, does not solve any problem. Immanence and transcendence are spatial symbols. God is *in* or *above* the world or both. The question is what does this mean in non-spatial terms? Certainly, God is neither in another nor in the same space as the world. He is the creative ground of the spatial structure of the world, but he is not bound to the structure, positively or negatively. The spatial symbol points to a qualitative relation: God is immanent in the world as its permanent creative ground and is transcendent to the world through freedom. Both infinite divinity and finite human freedom make the world transcendent to God and God transcendent to the world. The religious interest in the divine transcendence is not satisfied where one rightly asserts the infinite transcendence of the infinite over the finite. This transcendence does not contradict but rather confirms the coincidence of the opposites. This infinite is present in everything finite, in the stone, as well as in the genius. Transcendence demanded by religious experience is the freedom-to-freedom relationship which is actual in every personal encounter. Certainly, the holy is the 'quite other.' But the otherness is not really conceived as otherness if it remains in the aesthetic-cognitive realm and is not experienced as the otherness of the divine 'Thou,' whose freedom may conflict with my freedom. The meaning of the spatial symbols for the divine transcendence is the possible conflict and the possible reconciliation of infinite and finite freedom . . .

'The purpose of creation' is such an ambiguous concept that it should be avoided. Creation has no purpose beyond itself. From the point of view of the creature, the purpose of creation is the creature itself and the actualisation of its potentialities. From the point of view of the creator, the purpose of creation is the exercise of his creativity, which has no purpose beyond itself because the divine life is essentially creative. If 'the glory of God' is designated as the purpose of creation, as it is in Calvinist theologies, it is necessary, first of all, to understand the highly symbolic character of such a statement. No Calvinist theologian will admit that God lacks something which he must secure from the creature he has created. Such an idea is rejected as pagan. In creating the world, God is the sole cause of the glory he wishes to secure through his creation. But if he is the sole cause of his glory, he does not need the world to give him glory. He possesses it eternally in himself. In Lutheran theologies God's purpose is to have a communion of love with his creatures. God creates the world because the divine love wishes to have an object of love in addition to itself. Here again the implication is that God needs something he could not have without creation. Reciprocal love is interdependent love. Yet, according to Lutheran theology, there is nothing which the created world can offer God. He is the only one who gives.

The concept 'the purpose of creation' should be replaced by 'the *telos* of creativity' – the inner aim of fulfilling in actuality what is beyond potentiality and actuality in the divine life. One function of the divine creativity is to drive every creature toward such a fulfilment. Thus directing creativity must be added to originating and sustaining creation. It is the side of the divine creativity which is related to the future. The traditional term for directing creativity is 'providence.'

4.4 Creation after Barth

Per Lønning, *Creation: An Ecumenical Challenge?*, Macon, Georgia, Mercer University Press, 1989, pp. 13–16

To a large extent current tensions in the theology of creation reflect advocacy versus questioning of the Barthian inheritance. This observation may be almost as appropriate with regard to Roman Catholic theology as it is to Protestant theology. The emphatic Barthian 'no' to the Schleier-macher–Ritschl tradition is a 'no' to understanding the reality of God in terms of human consciousness, insisting instead on the Word as proclaiming a reality beyond the control of self-asserting subjective experience. This 'no' remains, however, in the line of that tradition when creation is approached not as the universal basis event objectively extending beyond the reach of the Christian confession, but as 'creation in Christ' and thus as a qualifier of Christian existence rather than as the concept carrying our total vision of the world.

Karl Barth's own exposition of creation theology in the third volume of his *Kirchliche Dogmatik* certainly shows no lack of interest in the notion of 'creation.' And subsequently some of the most striking contributions to the theme of creation have come from more or less proclaimed followers of Barth. In our day it may be meaningful to distinguish three trends of Barthian creation theology.

First, there is the super-Barthian view developed most characteristic-ally by Hans-Joachim Kraus in his *Systematische Theologie im Kontext biblisher Geschichte und Eschatologie*, in which 'God the Creator' (80–88) is programmatically and emphatically subordinate to 'The God of Israel Giving Testimony of His Coming' (52–137).

. . .

Whereas this must be seen as a vigorous reinforcement of Barth's *Heilsgeschichte* (history of salvation) approach to creation, professed neo Barthians like Eberhard Jüngel and Christian Link see a need to overcome a certain narrowness in the original Barthian approach by developing a conscious 'theology of nature.' In attempting to formulate the program of a new 'natural theology', Link emphatically rejects 'metaphysics' as 'inference from certain given "orders"', denies 'nature in its pure objectivity' as a source of intelligence, and focuses instead on the parables of Jesus as examples of a faith actively engaged in shaping reality, a real *credo ut intelligam* (Anselm of Canterbury: 'I believe in order to understand'). Jüngel's prescription for a new 'natural theology' goes very much in the same direction . . . roughly speaking, . . . that nature has nothing to say about God, but that the word of God has a good deal to say about nature – not about nature as a realm of reality cognizable prior to faith in Christ, but about 'nature' as a new vision of the universe constituted through the event of redemption in Christ.

The main exponent of a third post-Barthian trend is Jürgen Moltmann, with his comprehensive project of a Messianic theology:

Messianic theology is theology under the presupposition of the presence of the Messiah and the beginning of the Messianic era. On this presupposition, the Messianic understanding of the world is the true natural theology. (Moltmann, *God in Creation*, p. 60)

As opposed to the other authors quoted, Moltmann does not see that traditional natural theology is contradicted by the theology of revelation; rather, he understands the theology of revelation as a successor to and adaptation of traditional natural theology.

So pure *theologia naturalis* is theology under the conditions of pristine creation . . . in paradise. (p. 59)

Also for Moltmann, creation theology is but one aspect – albeit an integral aspect – of a vision that is totally oriented toward the history of salvation. There is, however, an obvious change in emphasis between his *Theologie der Hoffnung* (theology of hope) . . . and his more recent creation theology. His original point of reference, in addition to Barthian antimetaphysics, was Ernst Bloch's *Prinzip Hoffnung*, in which a basic concern is to liberate biblical apocalyptic vision from the bondage of biblical creation faith. The 'Behold, I make all things new' of the Apocalypse is a fiery protest against the 'Behold, it was very good' of Genesis. In Moltmann's theology, Bloch's idea of creation as a reactionary principle, committing the believers to authorize the present world as an expression of the Creator's will, is taken over and given a theologically challenging reinterpretation through a new and accentuated Trinitarian approach. Moltmann's Trinitarian doctrine of God refutes traditional monotheism, with its idea of creation as the work of one allegedly 'monolithic' Creator's will. Creation and Godhead are understood in a prominently Trinitarian way, as an interaction of Father, Son, and Spirit, and creation is seen within the framework of an all-comprehensive Messianic event. Although less pronounced than in Moltmann's earliest writings, the emphasis in this Messianic vision of history is still on the *adventus*, on God as the coming giver of future, but his reinforcement of the Trinitarian motif means that more equal weight is given to past and present as perspectives of the ongoing realization of our final hope.

When Moltmann gives his doctrine of creation the subtitle 'an ecological doctrine of creation,' it is, on the one hand, a sign of present-day involvement, namely that the ecological challenge is the setting for a truly contemporary theology of creation. On the other hand, it suggests a program of ecological awareness as a vision of the interrelatedness of all things. Even the divine, Trinitarian involvement with the world is not an interference from outside; rather it is an involvement *in* and *for* the created world. The most remarkable point about Moltmann's creation theology is probably how different emphases – more than one of which were originally obstructive to a substantial theology of creation – are combined and reinterpreted in light of a serious contemporary demand. The Barthian *Heilsgeschichte* scheme is preserved in principle, but doors are opened not only for an integration of scattered 'natural' observations but also for a seemingly pragmatic orientation based on a concern for the preservation of creation, a concern that is not and cannot be derived from a traditional soteriological approach to theology.

4.5 The goal of creation

Jürgen Moltmann, *God in Creation: An Ecological Doctrine of Creation*, ET London, SCM, 1985, pp. 196–7, 276–8

If we are interpreting the Christian belief in creation in the context of the knowledge of nature disclosed through evolutionary theory, we should bear the following points in mind:

1. Strictly speaking, evolution has nothing to do with 'creation' itself. It is concerned with the 'making' and 'ordering' of creation. Creating and making, creating and separating, are biblically distinct concepts which must not be confused. Creation is the term that describes the miracle of existence in general. The act of creation gathers into one single divine moment the whole of existence, even though this existence is in itself extended in time, and differentiated in its protean forms. Consequently there is in principle no contradiction between creation and evolution. The concepts belong on different levels. They are talking about different sides of the same reality.

2. Evolution describes the continued building up of matter and systems of life. This means that the theory of evolution has its place where theology talks about continuous creation (*creatio continua*). But how does God create and act in the ongoing history of creation? It is theologically wrong to transfer the forms of divine activity in the beginning to the forms of divine activity in history. Theologically we have to describe the forms through which God preserves, suffers, transforms and advances creation in their open-ended history – a history open to the future; though here the theological concept of openness to the future absorbs and transcends openness as the theory of a given system. In this respect our underlying theological premise must be that *creation is not*

yet finished, and has not as yet reached its end. In common with other forms of life and matter, the human being is involved in the open process of time. Today, the direct continuation of the evolution that led to the origin of the human species on earth lies in the hands of human beings themselves. They can either destroy this stage of evolution, or they can organize themselves into a higher form of common living than before, and advance evolution further.

3. The biblical – and especially the messianic – doctrine of creation fundamentally contradicts the picture of the static, closed cosmos, resting in its own equilibrium or revolving within itself. Its eschatological orientation towards a future consummation accords far more with the concept of a still incomplete *cosmic history*. But this means departing from the anthropocentric picture of the world. The human being is certainly the living thing with the highest development known to us. But 'the crown of creation' is God's sabbath. It is for this that human beings are created – for the feast of creation, which praises the eternal, inexhaustible God, and in this hymn of praise experiences and expresses its own joy. The enduring meaning of human existence lies in its *participation* in this joyful paean of God's creation. This song of praise was sung *before* the appearance of human beings, is sung *outside* the sphere of human beings, and will be sung even *after* human beings have – perhaps – disappeared from this planet. To put it without the images of biblical language: the human being is not the meaning and purpose of the world. The human being is not the meaning and purpose of evolution. The cosmogenesis is not bound to the destiny of human beings. The very reverse is true: the destiny of human beings is bound to the cosmogenesis. Theologically speaking, the meaning and purpose of human beings is to be found in God himself, like the meaning and purpose of all things. In this sense, every single person, and indeed every single living thing in nature, has a meaning, whether they are of utility for evolution or not. The meaning of the individual is not to be found in the collective of the species, and the meaning of the species is not to be found in the existence of the individual. The meaning of them both is to be found in God. Consequently no reduction is possible. All that is open to us is conciliating balance and mediation. We have to overcome the old anthropocentric world picture by a new theocentric interpretation of the world or nature of human beings, and by an eschatological understanding of the history of this natural and human world. Unless we do this, we shall not be able to find an adequate theological perspective for evolutionary theory.

. . .

The goal and completion of every Jewish and every Christian doctrine of creation must be the doctrine of the sabbath; for on the sabbath and through the sabbath God 'completed' his creation, and on the sabbath and through it, men and women perceive as God's creation the reality in which they live and which they themselves are. The sabbath opens creation for its true future. On the sabbath the redemption of the world is celebrated in anticipation. The sabbath is itself the presence of eternity in time, and a foretaste of the world to come. The observance of the sabbath became the identifying mark of Jews in exile; and in the same way, the doctrine of the sabbath of creation becomes the identifying mark of the biblical doctrine of creation, distinguishing it from the interpretation of the world as nature. It is the sabbath which manifests the world's identity as creation, sanctifies it and blesses it.

Curiously enough, in the Christian traditions, and especially the traditions of the Western church, creation is generally only presented as 'the six days' work'. The 'completion' of creation through 'the seventh day' is much neglected, or even overlooked altogether. It would seem as if Christian theology considered that both the sabbath commandment to Israel and the sabbath of creation were repealed and discarded when Jesus set aside the sabbath commandment by healing the sick on that day. As a result, God is viewed as the one who in his essential being is solely 'the creative God', as Paul Tillich says; and it follows from this that men and women too can only see themselves as this God's image if they become 'creative human beings'. The God who 'rests' on the sabbath, the blessing and rejoicing God, the God who delights in his creation, and in his exultation sanctifies it, recedes behind this different concept. So for men and women too, the meaning of their lives is identified with work and busy activity; and rest, the feast, and their joy in existence are pushed away, relegated to insignificance because they are non-utilitarian.

But according to the biblical traditions creation and the sabbath belong together. It is impossible to understand the world properly as creation without a proper discernment of the sabbath. In the sabbath stillness men and women no longer intervene in the environment through their labour. They let it be entirely God's creation. They recognize that as God's property creation is inviolable; and they sanctify the day through their joy in existence as God's creatures within the fellowship of creation.

The peace of the sabbath is peace with God first of all. But this divine peace encompasses not merely the soul but the body too; not merely individuals but family and people; not only human beings but animals as well; not living things alone, but also, as the creation story tells us, the whole creation of heaven and earth. That is why the sabbath peace is also the beginning of that peace with nature which many people are seeking today, in the face of the growing destruction of the environment. But there will never be peace with nature without the experience and celebration of God's sabbath.

If we look at the biblical traditions that have to do with the belief in creation, we discover that the sabbath is not a day of rest following six working days. On the contrary: the whole work of creation was performed *for the sake of the sabbath*. The sabbath is 'the feast of creation', as Franz Rosenzweig says. It was for the sake of this feast-day of the eternal God that heaven and earth were created, with everything that exists in them and lives. So although the creation story tells us that each day was followed by a night, God's sabbath knows no night but becomes the 'feast without end'.

The feast of creation is the feast of completion or consummation – the consummation of creation which is realized through this feast. Because this consummation of creation in the sabbath also represents creation's redemption – the redemption enabling it to participate in God's manifested, eternal presence – it will also be permissible for us to understand the sabbath as the feast of redemption. But if, as the feast of creation, it is also already the feast of creation's redemption, it is understandable that the whole of creation should have been brought into being for the sake of that redemption. 'The sabbath is the feast of creation', writes Franz Rosenzweig, 'but a creation which took place for the sake of the redemption. It is manifested at the end of creation, and manifested as creation's meaning and destination.'

4.6 Creation, sacrament and symbol

Per Lønning, *Creation: An Ecumenical Challenge?*, Macon, Georgia, Mercer University Press, 1989, pp. 45–6, 75, 231–4

The 'environmental crisis,' about which awareness began to grow in the late 1960s, very soon led to a questioning of Western Christianity (or even 'biblical religion' as such) about its role in a technological civilization based on a simple, instrumental consideration of nature. This was partly a negative echo to the claims of 'secular theology' in the immediately preceding period, for example, 'Creation as the Disenchantment of Nature,' 'The Exodus as the Desacralization of Politics', 'The Sinai Covenant as the Deconsecration of Values.' What the spokespersons of this theology considered to be the immortal glory of the Bible was exposed by the champions of the new ecological awareness as a betrayal of creation and a matchless seduction of humankind. The best-known critics were Lynn White, Jr. and Carl Amery, to whom it seemed clear that the three world religions rooted in the Bible – Judaism, Christianity, and Islam – had been the real agents in the promotion of a secularized vision of the world in that they stressed the transcendence of the Creator in such a way as to leave the earth at the ruthless exploitation of human hands. Most blame, however, was attributed to Christianity by virtue of its dominant political role in the modern world.

In face of this criticism Christian apologists hurried to admit that certain trends in Christian theology, as already pointed out by Max Weber, may well have exercised an exploitative influence, albeit due more to a distorted reading of the Bible – not least with regard to the 'Dominium terrae' of Genesis 1:28 – than to the Bible itself. Many observers, not least those speaking in the name of the Eastern churches, were particularly concerned to allocate the distortion to the Western theological tradition, where a pessimistic Augustinian vision of the corruption of nature was said to have combined with a disintegrative Scholastic overemphasis on conceptuality.

. . .

The following observation could have been made with little complex research: Contemporary stands by Christian churches on social issues are motivated *in some cases* by explicit or implicit *references to God the Creator* and to the universality of the Creator's design as obligatory to all; *in other cases* – by far the most numerous – they are motivated by *references to redemption* as a particular divine action within history, obligatory – at least at first glance – only to that selected portion of humankind who, individually or corporately, has become involved with that (salvation) history. The theological weakness of the first orientation is that it tends to see that Christians are no more concerned than the rest of humankind in general; the weakness of the second is that it tends to see that ethical imperatives are reserved exclusively for Christians, for it indicates no reason for concern on the part of people who are unfamiliar with the biblical *Heilsgeschichte*. Correspondingly, both have their merits: *the one* underlines the Creator's design as a pattern that is obligatory to all humankind (and all creation) and, to some extent, even operative in all, be they conscious of it or not; *the other* highlights the motivating force of the Christ event and thus reminds Christians that their focal commitment is faithfulness to Christ. The competitive as well as the constructive tension of these two orientations is bound to keep appearing in a study on the ecumenical implications of Christian creation faith today.

. . .

[In] the late Archbishop of Canterbury, William Temple['s] . . . Gifford Lectures (1933–1934), *Nature, Man and God*, . . . the chapter that has exercised the most remarkable influence, particularly in recent years, is the one on 'The Sacramental Universe.' Even if this series of lectures represents a conscious effort to stay within the limits of 'natural theology' and makes no claim to any (and depends on no) presupposition founded in special revelation, this chapter very much focuses on aspects that are more specific to Christianity than to any other religion. However, Temple remains faithful to his enterprise in that he does not see it as his task to preach the gospel of incarnation and sacramental presence; rather he intends to show how these claims relate meaningfully to a rational con-templation of the cosmos. In the meantime, however, and particularly during the last 15 years, the very concept of a 'sacramental universe,' introduced for the first time by that book, has acquired tremendous influence not only in Anglican theology but throughout ecumenical theological reflection.

. . .

Temple introduces his famous formula as follows:

We are trying to frame a conception which is not identical with any of the commonly offered suggestions concerning the relation of the eternal to the historical, and are now extending its application so as to include the relation of the spiritual and the material . . . and there is in some religious traditions an element which is . . . so close akin to what we want that we may most suitably call this . . . the sacramental conception.

We are now . . . concerned . . . to vindicate the principle on which belief in sacraments reposes, in order that we may be secure in using it as a clue to the understanding of the relation of spirit to matter in the universe.

Thus the view of the universe which I have called sacramental asserts the supremacy and absolute freedom of God. . . . Matter exists in its full reality but at a secondary level. It is created by spirit – the Divine Spirit – to be the vehicle of spirit and the sphere of spirit's self-realization in and through the activity of controlling it. (pp. 481–2, 485, 493)

. . .

Forty years after Temple's proposition concerning the 'sacramental universe', Peacocke, oriented less toward philosophy and more toward natural science, arrives at a more concise theory than the late archbishop:

> The created world is seen by Christians as a symbol because it is a mode of God's revelation. . . . It is also valued by them for what God is effecting instrumentally through it, what he does for men in and through it. But these two functions of matter, the symbolical and the instrumental, also constitute the special character of the use of matter in the particular Christian sacraments. Hence there is, in each particular sacrament, a universal reference to this double character of created physical reality and, correspondingly, meaning can be attached to speaking of the created world as a sacrament or, at least, as sacramental. However, it must be recognized that this sacramental character is only implicit, and that it is obscure and partial both because of man's limited perception and sensitivity and because of evil. The significance of the incarnation of God in a man within the created world is that in the incarnate Christ the sacramental character of that world was made explicit and perfected. In this sense, it may seem legitimate to regard the incarnate life of Christ as the supreme sacrament. (In H. Montefiore (ed.), *Man and Nature*, 1975, London, Collins, pp. 133–4)

4.7 A Christian meditation on creation

Pierre Teilhard de Chardin, *Hymn of the Universe*, ET London, Collins, 1965, pp. 19–21

Since once again, Lord – though this time not in the forests of the Aisne but in the steppes of Asia – I have neither bread, nor wine, nor altar, I will raise myself beyond these symbols, up to the pure majesty of the real itself; I, your priest, will make the whole earth my altar and on it will offer you all the labours and sufferings of the world.

Over there, on the horizon, the sun has just touched with light the outermost fringe of the eastern sky. Once again, beneath this moving sheet of fire, the living surface of the earth wakes and trembles, and once again begins its fearful travail. I will place on my paten, O God, the harvest to be won by this renewal of labour. Into my chalice I shall pour all the sap which is to be pressed out this day from the earth's fruits.

My paten and my chalice are the depths of a soul laid widely open to all the forces which in a moment will rise up from every corner of the earth and converge upon the Spirit. Grant me the remembrance and the mystic presence of all those whom the light is now awakening to the new day.

One by one, Lord, I see and I live all those whom you have given me to sustain and charm my life. One by one also I number those who make up that other beloved family which has gradually surrounded me, its unity fashioned out of the most disparate elements, with affinities of the heart, of scientific research, and of thought. And again one by one – more vaguely it is true, yet all-inclusively – I call before me the whole vast anonymous army of living humanity; those who surround me and support me though I do not know them; those who come, and those who go; above all, those who in office, laboratory and factory, through their vision of truth or despite their error, truly believe in the progress of earthly reality and who today will take up again their impassioned pursuit of the light.

This restless multitude, confused or orderly, the immensity of which terrifies us; this ocean of humanity whose slow, monotonous wave-flows trouble the hearts even of those whose faith is most firm: it is to this deep that I thus desire all the fibres of my being should respond. All the things in the world to which this day will bring increase; all those that will diminish, all those too that will die: all of them, Lord, I try to gather into my arms, so as to hold them out to you in offering. This is the material of my sacrifice; the only material you desire.

Once upon a time men took into your temple the first fruits of their harvests, the flower of their flocks. But the offering you really want, the offering you mysteriously need every day to appease your hunger, to slake your thirst is nothing less than the growth of the world borne ever onwards in the stream of universal becoming.

Receive, O Lord, this all-embracing host which your whole creation, moved by your magnetism, offers you at this dawn of a new day.

This bread, our toil, is of itself, I know, but an immense fragmentation; this wine, our pain, is no more, I know, than a draught that dissolves. Yet in the very depths of this formless mass you have implanted – and this I am sure of, for I sense it – a desire, irresistible, hallowing, which makes us cry out, believer and unbeliever alike: 'Lord, make us *one*.'

Because, my God, though I lack the soul-zeal and the sublime integrity of your saints, I yet have received from you an overwhelming sympathy for all that stirs within the dark mass of matter; because I know myself to be irremediably less a child of heaven than a son of earth; therefore I will this morning climb up in spirit to the high places, bearing with me the hopes and the miseries of my mother; and there – empowered by that priesthood which you alone (as I firmly believe) have bestowed on me – upon all that in the world of human flesh is now about to be born or to die beneath the rising sun I will call down the Fire.

Topics for discussion

1 What is the relation between creation and redemption? Was Barth (supported by the Roman Catholic theologian Baum) right to assert that creation is known only through redemption, or does such a claim undermine other important truths e.g. the universality of conscience and natural law?

2 Can there be a *Christian* doctrine of creation? What would be its emphases?

3 Is Moltmann's use of the sabbath to stress the future direction of creation sufficient to overcome Bloch's objection that the doctrine of creation merely reinforces the status quo, or should the doctrine of creation be defended from such attacks in some other way?

4 To what extent is Christianity to blame for our present environmental crisis? Might a more sacramental view of matter have helped?

Acknowledgements

HarperCollins for quotations from the New Revised Standard Version of the Bible; SCM Press for quotations from *Principles of Christian Theology* by John Macquarrie and *Creation and Temptation* by Dietrich Bonhoeffer; Darton Longman & Todd Ltd for a quotation from *The Openness of Being: Natural Theology Today* by Eric L. Mascall; James Nisbet & Co Ltd for a quotation from *Doctrines of the Creed: Their Basis in Scripture and Their Meaning Today* by Oliver Chase Quick; HarperCollins Publishers Inc for quotations from *God in Creation: A New Theology of Creation and the Spirit of God* by Jürgen Moltmann, English translation copyright © 1985 SCM Press Ltd; Pearson Education for quotations from *Issues in Science and Religion* by Ian G. Barbour; Church House Publishing for quotations from *We Believe in the Holy Spirit* copyright © The Archbishops' Council 1991; Blackwell Publishers Ltd for quotations from *Invitation to Theology* and *Continental Philosophy and Modern Theology: An Engagement* (both) by David Brown and 'Process Theology' by Kenneth Surin in *The Modern Theologians: An Introduction to Christian Theology in the Twentieth Century*, II edited by David F. Ford; quotation from D. Basinger reprinted by permission from *Divine Power and Process Theism* edited by James R. Lewis, the State University of New York Press. © 1988 State University of New York. All rights reserved; Schubert M. Ogden for a quotation from *The Reality of God and Other Essays* by Schubert M. Ogden; John B. Cobb Jr and The Lutterworth Press for quotations from *A Christian Natural Theology: Based on the Thought of Alfred North Whitehead* by John B. Cobb Jr; the estate of Colin Gunton for a quotation from *Becoming & Being*; Wm B. Eerdmans Publishing Co for a quotation from *God, Action and Embodiment* by Thomas F. Tracy © 1984 Wm B. Eerdmans Publishing Co, Grand Rapids, Michigan; Orbis Books for a quotation from 'The Spirituality of the Earth' by Thomas Berry in *Liberating Life: Contemporary Approaches to Ecological Theology* edited by Charles Birch, William Eakin and Jay B. McDaniel; *New Blackfriars* for a quotation from 'Biology and Theology in Conversation: Reflections on Ecological Theology' in *New Blackfriars*

74(865), 1993; Continuum for quotations from Carol J. Adams's Introduction to *Ecofeminism and the Sacred* edited by Carol J. Adams, *How to Think about the Earth: Philosophical and Theological Models for Ecology* by Stephen R.L. Clark and *Church Dogmatics* I, 1, III, 1 and IV, 1 by Karl Barth; Stephen R.L. Clark for a quotation from 'Is Nature God's Will?' in *Animals on the Agenda: Questions about Animals for Theology and Ethics* edited by Andrew Linzey and Dorothy Yamamoto; the Domestic and Foreign Missionary Society of the Protestant Episcopal Church USA for a quotation from *Man Becoming: God in Secular Experience* by Gregory Baum; The University of Chicago Press for a quotation from *Systematic Theology*, I by Paul Tillich; Mercer University Press for quotations from *Creation: An Ecumenical Challenge* by Per Lønning and Editions du Seuil for a quotation from *Hymne à l'universie* by Pierre Teilhard de Chardin © Editions du Seuil 1961.

Further reading

Introductory and general

Astley, J. (2000) *God's World*, London, Darton, Longman & Todd.

Barth, K. (1966) *Dogmatics in Outline*, ET London, SCM, Chs 8 and 9.

Brümmer, V. (ed.) (1991) *Interpreting the Universe as Creation*, Kampen, Kok Pharos.

Gunton, C. (1997) 'The Doctrine of Creation', in C. E. Gunton (ed.), *The Cambridge Companion to Christian Doctrine*, Cambridge, Cambridge University Press, pp. 141–7.

Kaufman, G. D. (1978) *Systematic Theology: A Historicist Perspective*, New York, Scribners, Ch. 20.

Macquarrie, J. (1966, 1977) *Principles of Christian Theology*, London, SCM, Ch. X.

Migliore, D. L. (1991) *Faith Seeking Understanding: An Introduction to Christian Theology*, Grand Rapids, MI, Eerdmans, Ch. 5.

Montefiore, H. (ed.) (1975) *Man and Nature*, London, Collins.

Page, R. (1996) *God and the Web of Creation*, London, SCM.

Quick, O. C. (1963) *Doctrines of the Creed: Their Basis in Scripture and their Meaning Today*, London, Collins, Ch. V.

Thomas, O. C. (1983) *Introduction to Theology*, Wilton, CT, Morehouse, Ch. 6.

Vanstone, W. H. (1977) *Love's Endeavour, Love's Expense: The Response of Being to the Love of God*, London, Darton, Longman & Todd, Ch. 2.

Ward, K. (1996) *Religion and Creation*, Oxford, Oxford University Press.

Westermann, C. (1974) *Creation*, ET London, SPCK.

1 Creation: What does it mean?

Barbour, I. G. (1966) *Issues in Science and Religion*, London, SCM.

Barbour, I. G. (ed.) (1968) *Science and Religion: New Perspectives on the Dialogue*, London, SCM, Part 3.

Barbour, I. G. (1990) *Religion in an Age of Science*, London, SCM.

Church of England Doctrine Commission (1991) *We Believe in the Holy Spirit*, London, Church House Publishing.

Davies, P. C. W. (1987) *The Cosmic Blueprint*, London, Unwin.

Gilkey, L. (1959) *Maker of Heaven and Earth*, New York, Doubleday.

Gunton, C. E. (ed.) (1997) *The Doctrine of Creation: Essays in Dogmatics, History and Philosophy*, Edinburgh, T & T Clark.

Hefner, P. J. (1984) 'The Creation', in C. E. Braaten and R. W. Jenson (eds), *Christian Dogmatics*, 1, Philadelphia, Fortress, pp. 265–357.

Mascall, E. L. (1956) *Christian Theology and Natural Science: Some Questions on their Relations*, London, Longmans, Green, Ch. 4.

Montenat, C., Plateaux, L. and Roux, P. (1985) *How to Read the World: Creation in Evolution*, ET London, SCM.

Peacocke, A. R. (1979) *Creation and the World of Science*, Oxford, Oxford University Press.

Polkinghorne, J. (1994) *Science and Christian Belief: Theological Reflections of a Bottom-up Thinker*, London, SPCK, Ch. 4.

Ruse, M. (2001) *Can a Darwinian be a Christian? The Relationship between Science and Religion*, Cambridge, Cambridge University Press.

Santmire, H. P. (1985) *The Travail of Nature: The Ambiguous Ecological Promise of Christian Theology*, Minneapolis, MN, Fortress.

Southgate, C. *et al.* (1999) *God, Humanity and the Cosmos: A Textbook in Science and Religion*, Edinburgh, T & T Clark.

Temple, W. (1953) *Nature, Man and God*, London, Macmillan.

Ward, K. (1996) *God, Chance and Necessity*, Oxford, Oneworld.

Woods, G. F. (1958) *Theological Explanation*, Welwyn, Nisbet, Ch. XV.

2 Process theology: A more engaging God?

Basinger, D. (1988) *Divine Power in Process Theism: A Philosophical Critique*, New York, State University of New York Press.

Birch, L. C. (1965) *Nature and God*, London, SCM.

Brown, D., James, R. E. and Reeves, G. (eds) (1971) *Process Philosophy and Christian Thought*, Indianapolis, IN, Bobbs-Merrill.

Cobb, J. B. (1966) *A Christian Natural Theology: Based on the Thought of Alfred North Whitehead*, London, Lutterworth.

Cobb, J. B. and Griffin, D. R. (1977) *Process Theology: An Introductory Exposition*, Belfast, Christian Journals.

Fiddes, P. S. (1993) 'Process Theology', in A. E. McGrath (ed.), *The Blackwell Encyclopedia of Modern Christian Thought*, Oxford, Blackwell, pp. 472–6.

Gunton, C. (1978) *Becoming and Being: The Doctrine of God in Charles Hartshorne and Karl Barth*, Oxford, Oxford University Press.

Hartshorne, C. (1976) *The Divine Relativity: A Social Conception of God*, New Haven, CT, Yale University Press.

Hartshorne, C. and Reese, W. L. (eds) (1953) *Philosophers Speak of God*, Chicago, University of Chicago Press.

Ogden, S. (1977) *The Reality of God and Other Essays*, San Francisco, Harper and Row.

Pailin, D. A. (1986) *Groundwork of Philosophy of Religion*, London, Epworth, Chs 6 and 7.

Pailin, D. A. (1989) *God and the Processes of Reality: Foundations of a Credible Theism*, London, Routledge.

Pittenger, N. (1968) *Process Thought and Christian Faith*, London, SCM.

Pittenger, N. (1969) *Alfred North Whitehead*, London, Lutterworth.

Surin, K. (1989) 'Process Theology', in D. Ford (ed.), *The Modern Theologians*, II, Oxford, Blackwell, pp. 103–14.

Tracy, T. F. (1984) *God, Action, and Embodiment*, Grand Rapids, MI, Eerdmans.

Whitehead, A. N. (1926) *Religion in the Making*, Cambridge, Cambridge University Press.

3 God or Gaia? The environmental challenge

Birch, C., Eakin, W. and McDaniel, J. B. (eds) (1990), *Liberating Life: Contemporary Approaches to Ecological Theology*, Maryknoll, New York, Orbis.

Botkin, D. (1990) *Discordant Harmonies*, New York, Oxford University Press.

Clark, S. R. L. (1993) *How to Think about the Earth: Philosophical and Theological Models for Ecology*, London, Mowbray.

Cooper, T. (1990) *Green Christianity: Caring for the Whole Creation*, Sevenoaks, Hodder & Stoughton.

Deane-Drummond, C. (1996) *A Handbook in Theology and Ecology*, London, SCM.

Deane-Drummond, C. (2001) *Biology and Theology Today: Exploring the Boundaries*, London, SCM, Chs 7 and 8.

Gray, E. D. (1979) *Green Paradise Lost*, Wellesley, MA, Roundtable.

Halkes, C. J. M. (1991) *New Creation: Christian Feminism and the Renewal of the Earth*, London, SPCK.

Hodgson, P. C. (1994) *Winds of the Spirit: A Constructive Christian Theology*, London, SCM, Chs 6 and 7.

Jantzen, G. M. (1984) *God's World, God's Body*, London, Darton, Longman & Todd.

Linzey, A. and Yamamoto, D. (eds) (1998) *Animals on the Agenda: Questions about Animals for Theology and Ethics*, London, SCM.

Lovelock, J. (1988) *The Ages of Gaia: A Biography of Our Living Earth*, Oxford, Oxford University Press.

McFague, S. (1987) *Models of God: Theology for an Ecological, Nuclear Age*, London, SCM, especially Ch. 3.

McFague, S. (1993) *The Body of God: An Ecological Theology*, Minneapolis, MN, Fortress.

Meeker, J. W. (1988) *Minding the Earth: Thinly Disguised Essays on Human Ecology*, Alameda, CA, Latham Foundation.

Moltmann, J. (1985) *God in Creation: An Ecological Doctrine of Creation*, ET London, SCM.

Ruether, R. R. (1975) *New Woman/New Earth: Sexist Ideologies and Human Liberation*, New York, Seabury.

Ruether, R. R. (1992) *Gaia and God: An Ecofeminist Theology of Earth Healing*, London, SCM.

Russell, C. A. (1994) *The Earth, Humanity and God*, London, UCL Press.

Santmire, H. P. (1985) *The Travail of Nature: The Ambiguous Ecological Promise*, Minneapolis, MN, Fortress.

Tanner, K. (1988) *God and Creation in Christian Theology: Tyranny or Empowerment*, Oxford, Blackwell.

Warren, K. J. (1990) 'The Power and Promise of Ecological Feminism', *Environmental Ethics*, 12, 3, pp. 125–46.

Young, R. A. (1994) *Healing the Earth: A Theocentric Perspective on Environmental Problems and their Solutions*, Nashville, TN, Broadman & Holman.

4 Christian creation?

Barth, K. (1958) *Church Dogmatics*, III, 1, ET Edinburgh, T & T Clark.

Brunner, E. (1952) *The Christian Doctrine of Creation and Redemption*, ET London, Lutterworth.

Lønning, P. (1989) *Creation: An Ecumenical Challenge?*, Macon, GA, Mercer University Press.

Moltmann, J. (1985) *God in Creation: An Ecological Doctrine of Creation*, ET London, SCM.

Montefiore, H. (ed.) (1975) *Man and Nature*, London, Collins.

Muddiman, J. (1998) 'A New Testament Doctrine of Creation?', in A. Linzey and D. Yamamoto (eds), *Animals on the Agenda: Questions about Animals for Theology and Ethics*, London, SCM, pp. 25–34.

Temple, W. (1953) *Nature, Man and God*, London, Macmillan.

Tillich, P. (1953) *Systematic Theology*, I, London, Nisbet.

Ward, K. (1996) *Religion and Creation*, Oxford, Oxford University Press, Part IV.

Young, N. (1976) *Creator, Creation and Faith*, London, Collins, Ch. 7.

Index of subjects

Index of names